A Horseman's Progress

Charles Wilson

Published 2007 by arima publishing

www.arimapublishing.com

ISBN 978 1 84549 262 5

© Charles Wilson 2007

All rights reserved

This book is copyright. Subject to statutory exception and to provisions of relevant collective licensing agreements, no part of this publication may be reproduced, stored in a retrieval system, or transmitted in any form or by any means, without the prior written permission of the author.

Printed and bound in the United Kingdom

Typeset in Garamond 11/14

This book is sold subject to the conditions that it shall not, by way of trade or otherwise, be lent, re-sold, hired out, or otherwise circulated without the publisher's prior consent in any form of binding or cover other than that which it is published and without a similar condition including this condition being imposed on the subsequent purchaser.

arima publishing
ASK House, Northgate Avenue
Bury St Edmunds, Suffolk IP32 6BB
t: (+44) 01284 700321

www.arimapublishing.com

I dedicate this book to the late Thea Macfarlane who taught me so much and could have taught much more. For her it all came naturally.

Acknowledgements:

To Rachel Bedingfield, Abi Hogg and Paula Cox who encouraged my first faltering attempts. To Sarah Todd, who first cast her eye on the finished script, giving invaluable help with presentation and grammar. To Sue Rotheram, Mike Lawson and Jayne Lavender for their perceptive suggestions. To Sheril Leich for her help and guidance about publishing. To Liz Molyneux whose enthusiasm and marketing expertise kept the whole project on course.

Finally to my wife Judith, who fanned the flames of an idea into a book and made it all possible.

CONTENTS

Introduction	7
About this Book	11
Chapter One - Trust	13
Chapter Two - Understanding	27
Chapter Three - Leadership	45
Chapter Four - Systems	59
Chapter Five - Balance the Bodies	77
Chapter Six - Release and Reward	89
Chapter Seven - Time	107
Chapter Eight - Connecting and Feel	127
Selected Bibliography	149

Introduction

My equine upbringing in the fifties was not perhaps typical of the time seeing that I was a 'townie'. Ours was an academic family, my father being a lecturer at Liverpool University. We lived in the heart of suburbia in the quiet dormitory town of West Kirby. The first horse I rode, aged eight, was Dolphin and I was terrified. This was at the small riding school nearby, run by Glyn Blakeley and her daughter Wendy; this was a green oasis amidst the grey and brown of the town. Here I received a good traditional grounding in riding and horse care. Mrs Blakeley was not one to suffer fools gladly and I quickly learnt what was an acceptable standard. Lessons in the school were not half as much fun as riding out, especially along the beach. This was a mile on the sands, either out to sea at low tide or along the shore towards Hoylake. Whichever way, it usually became a desperate effort not to be galloped flat out back to the slipway. I quickly learnt how to jam my pony's head six inches behind the backside of the one in front. These were years of gentle learning and fun.

This good start was furthered at Thea and Donald Macfarlane's riding school and Highland pony stud near Dunblane, Scotland. I was thirteen when I went for a riding holiday, beginning a lifelong friendship. Mr and Mrs Mac were an ideal partnership, he was a brilliant teacher and she was a natural horsewoman. Her forthright personality cared only for the welfare of the horses, both in their management and when ridden. Under her tutelage I was exposed to an exacting standard of horsemanship. Mrs Mac had been trained in the twenties and thirties by two high class horse dealers, Captains Jack and Bob Knight. Their traditional ex army ways were passed directly to us students. Even now, if I am stuck with a difficult horse, I think what Mrs Mac would have done.

In 1968 I went up to St. Catharine's College, Cambridge to read Geography. I joined the newly formed riding club and expanded my riding skills, culminating in team captain in my final year. The inter-university competitions quickly tested one's horsemanship as both teams rode the same horses, just having twenty minutes to achieve a degree of rapport before the dressage test or jumping round. During my last two years at university I spent time exercising a local farmer's point-to-point horses. This was instrumental in my decision not to use my degree in a subject related career but rather pursue one with horses. This was further endorsed after spending three months in Holland working for Henri Gilhuys, a well respected dressage trainer. My interest had always lain in schooling and smoothing away at a horse's rough edges, so I envisaged my future would be in dressage or showing. However Major Derek Allhusen, the university club's president, advised me not to specialise too soon. Consequently I enrolled for a stud management course at Derisley Wood near Newmarket. This was an eye opener to see a large commercial operation in the high flying world of horse racing. After a year it was time to move on.

The way of learning in the horse world then, and still now to a certain extent, was to serve your apprenticeship. This meant working for almost nothing to learn and gain experience. I reasoned that as the pay and conditions would be the same everywhere I might as well give my services to the best. Thus I wrote to the leading showing, dressage and eventing trainers; from half a dozen letters I was offered two interviews. As a result in 1972 I started work for Colonel V.D.S. Williams at East Burnham Park. One of the leading horsemen of the C20th, a founder of the British Horse Society, he devoted his life to improving the quality of training and riding in Britain. He brought Colonel Podhajsky, from the Spanish Riding School of Vienna, over to his home to help the fledgling dressage movement. He provided facilities for and helped train several Olympic eventing teams. His wife Brenda had represented Britain at the Rome Olympics. His knowledge of horses and the horse world was incomparable and I felt privileged to work for him. Then in his eighties he had started a new enterprise, importing an Appaloosa stallion and several broodmares from Canada. It was with these that I was to work; handling and backing the young stock under the guidance of the Colonel and Griselda the stud groom. The most interesting times were the long conversations I had with the Colonel about horsemanship and the colourful characters he had met in his lifetime. Unfortunately he died the following year; however the classical grounding he imparted has never left me.

A year later I began working for myself. This was a time of building on what I had learnt, taking in horses for backing and schooling, and bringing on my own with a view to going eventing. By the early eighties I had bought a dairy farm in Yorkshire combining this with the horse work. I had a very good horse Millstone Lad who took me both eventing and pointing, culminating in the Bramham three day event. If that was the icing on the cake the bread and butter was still backing and bringing on young horses.

INTRODUCTION

My wife Judith has always had a passion for coloured horses and in the late eighties my life moved in this direction with the purchase of Phillip Pembroke. He began showing as a yearling and such was his success and marvellous temperament I decided to keep him as a stallion. He won numerous showing championships, took me hunting for seven seasons, went team chasing and competed up to medium level in dressage. He stood at stud for ten years before succumbing to an acute attack of laminitis. Once bitten with the coloured horse bug I just had to find another, so in 2001 I bought Icon's Image, an athletic skewbald warm blood who is the current resident stallion.

Although passing the B.H.S.A.I exam in my youth I did little teaching until the 1990's, viewing the intervening years as a time of accruing knowledge and experience. What surprised me was that there were many people unaware of the basics that a horse needs from the rider in terms of seat and training. I now teach on a daily basis and travel all over the country.

Another milestone was my introduction to natural horsemanship in the late nineties. Of course there is nothing natural about riding - it would not be the horse's choice. My first introduction was through Pat Parelli. My immediate reaction was that he made obvious sense; he put the psychological side of horse handling in a readily understandable and accessible format. In many ways this was a reflection of what my early teachers, Thea Macfarlane and Colonel Williams, had done without thinking. I spent some time studying in Colorado with Pat. Other proponents of natural horsemanship with whom I have worked are Australians Ken Faulkner and Jayne Lavender. I regularly teach with Jayne when she is in Britain. To some the very phrase natural horsemanship and its promotion are provocative and challenging. For me there is good and bad in many different approaches, it is all a matter of personal interpretation and execution.

I also regularly write in the 'Your Horse' magazine as an equine agony uncle. This more than anything has brought home to me the gaps in many peoples' basic understanding of how and why a horse thinks, feels and behaves.

This is where I am today - still competing in the dressage and show rings - backing and schooling - standing a coloured stallion - teaching people how to handle and ride horses with understanding and feeling.

About this book

This book is intended for everybody who cares about horses.

> It is about horsemanship.
> It will show you how to understand horses.
> It will help you how to handle horses safely and happily.
> It will show you how to give your horse what he needs so he too can feel safe and happy.

As the title suggests this is a continual learning process and one that must include the horse. As in any partnership there will be ups and downs, after all we are dealing with two different species. However an understanding of what makes a horse 'tick' and how to tune into his wavelength can smooth the path.

This is not a specific 'how to do book'. There are many excellent ones, but unfortunately they start by assuming you have a horse that is in a receptive mental and physical condition. From my experience this is not so for many of today's riders. I see horses that are dull and withdrawn; or anxious and confused; or pushy and bargy. They may be manageable to a certain degree, but for many it could be so much better with a little more understanding and knowledge. Some people enjoy the challenge of a 'work out' with a horse. However most of us just want a horse that is pleasant to handle and ride so that we can pursue our chosen discipline with enjoyment. Of course this is what our horse would like as well. So in effect much of this book is about is getting the horse to where he is trainable; although all the concepts apply whatever level the partnership.

There are three aspects to each chapter. The first is one of concepts, reflecting that chapter's title. I have kept these short and thus memorable. Secondly the theme is then illustrated with a couple of case studies. Details of what and how to do are given in these specific instances. Please understand they only applied to that person and horse at that moment in time. Still as a guide they may be of some help. The horses and people are all real, although the names have been changed. As far as memory serves the events unfolded as written and I would like to thank the participants for their assistance in furthering the cause of horsemanship. Finally the chapter's theme is loosely followed in an anecdotal way. In John Bunyan's classic - 'The Pilgrim's Progress - the hero Christian journeys to the Celestial City with many trials and tribulations on the way. I am still travelling on my progress. Unlike Christian I will never arrive as one does not stop learning. It is the journey that is important.

The presumption to believe that I have learnt anything worth imparting comes from feeling an affinity with the struggling student. Not being a 'natural' I have had to learn from many mistakes and I continue to do so.

Chapter One

TRUST

'Wherefore Christian was left to tumble in the Slough of Despond alone'
(The Pilgrims Progress - John Bunyan)

The horseman sat in the corner of the school, a blanket over his knees, a scarf around his neck, a fur hat on his head; it was a cold December morning. The young man was lungeing an unbacked three year old, called Rose. The head girl was standing watching, she had already worked her youngster. Today the horseman had said he could lean over the mare.

The preparation had been thorough. Rose had been taught to lead in hand. She would willingly walk and trot around the arena just from the voice. She had become used to wearing a saddle; she had not bucked at all. She was led with a line from the lungeing cavesson, but had a jointed snaffle in her mouth. She had got used to it during the last ten days. She did not even mind the long side reins, which were attached to the bit. They only came into play when she reached down with her head and neck. This was a comfortable position, where she could get used to feeling the reins against the bit in her mouth. It was a shock the first time, she learnt if she lifted her head she could not feel them, but that wasn't very comfortable either. Gradually in the last few days she had discovered, if she lowered her head to where it was comfortable she could feel the bit but it did not hurt unless she pushed against it. Anyway it was never for very long and there was a feed at the end. She had learnt to trot and even canter and change direction. She had learnt the voice commands; he had learnt to lift the whip if she did not understand and how to lower it when she did. He was looking forward to backing her. He felt excited, at last the rather boring lungeing would be over and soon riding would start. He was not worried; after all at his last stables he had backed a horse, his first.

The girl held Rose for him and petted her; she was one of her favourites. He stood on the mounting block while she led the mare past, several times in both directions. The mare did not mind she was content to stand still, but she did twitch her ears and lift her head when he reached over and gingerly touched the saddle. He did it again several times; she swung round and rolled her eyes alarmingly. The more he persisted the worse she became. Now she would no longer stand near the block at all.

The horseman said, 'maybe she's not as ready as I thought'. So they finished when the mare would stand quietly if he did not move. The horseman's disappointment was masked with iron discipline; he could only bear the cold for an hour at a time. 'We'll try again tomorrow', he said.

He tried not to look at the head girl's big reproachful eyes. He hadn't done anything the horseman had not told him, this mare did not seem to be the same as the other one he'd backed.

The next day was the same. The mare lunged perfectly; she stood by the block quietly. As he waited to lean over her he wondered if she would fidget like yesterday. No she was worse, as soon as he stretched out his hand to touch her, let alone the saddle, she leapt away and this time would not be led back. He could see the head girl was dying to say something, but she kept quiet, just stroking and soothing the mare. He could see the horseman huddled stiffly in the corner, his shoulders sagging with the cold but also with disappointment and frustration. There was a time when the old man could have walked over and got straight on that mare. Now he knew he had to teach this boy how to do it. He barked gruffly,

'I can't let you ruin that mare, tomorrow swap horses, Daffodil will be easier. Rose does not trust you'. The girl brightened with relief but tried not to show it; she did not want to hurt his feelings.

He felt the bottom drop out of his world. Why wouldn't the mare let him near? He had done everything according to the book. What's more he just knew the girl would have no trouble tomorrow. Why didn't the horseman say more? Perhaps Rose wouldn't trust the girl either. The girl never seemed to do very much, she was so quiet with the horses it was a wonder they could hear her. She did not use her voice the way he did, with clear changes of tone. She hardly moved at all, only a little lift of her shoulders for them to go on and a sag in her body for them to slow down.

The boy went to bed crestfallen and resentful. His journey was just starting.

HARRY

I gently eased myself into the saddle and sat doing nothing. It is always a big step in restarting a horse however much preparation you have done. It had taken ten minutes before Harry would stand quietly at the mounting block. I had to reposition him each time he moved. It was essential that he would stand still, with the reins dropped on his neck, and accept me standing ready to mount. Harry was a big warm blood cross, over 17hh, but also one of the most frightened and mistrustful horses I had ever come across. When he arrived he was literally scared of nearly everything.

His owner Jill had rung me after she was at her wits end. Her story was similar to so many others, but in this case more extreme. She had ridden since childhood and had got to the stage of wanting to start eventing. She had outgrown her earlier horses or they were not athletic enough for today's job; a local dealer seemed to have just what she needed. Harry looked like an old fashioned steeplechaser, big and rangy with plenty of potential, 5 yrs old and ready to bring on. He looked a bit thin, but then it was early spring and maybe he had not wintered well. The dealer showed him off. He tucked his nose in, went through his paces, popped a couple of jumps and did the same for Jill, the deal was done. It was when he went to Jill's yard that things changed; within a day the calmness had worn off, the horse had turned into a jumpy nervous animal. Out riding he was spooky and becoming harder to control. The final straw was when, for no apparent reason, he bolted down the lane and headed for the dual carriageway; only a bend in the road and a conveniently open gateway prevented a major accident. Jill had then tried schooling indoors but there he would get worked up and start bucking. Jill was rapidly losing her confidence and when she contacted me she had not ridden him for two months.

As he stepped out of the trailer I could see he was big, weak and gangly. His face told me most, he had a big honest eye but it looked sad and not what I call, 'out into the world'. There were worry lines above his eyes and tightness around his lips. I approached to let him sniff my hand, he took little interest. However as soon as I raised my hand to stroke his shoulder he leapt sideways and whirled round me. 'Don't worry', I said 'let's put him in the field and let him settle, we'll start him tomorrow'.

I caught him next day, without trouble. I had a long lead rope; I didn't want him to feel constricted. I watched him closely as we walked to the yard. His ears flickered, his head went up a fraction and the next moment he had nearly landed on top of me. At first I couldn't see what had frightened him, then I saw our dog in the hedge back a 100 yards away - this horse really was on his guard. In the stable he was fine, you could brush him, handle his feet, all the usual things; because there he felt secure.

I started working him in the school just with a halter and a long rope. He was the biggest scaredy cat I had met. Frightened of any movement in the fields around the arena, frightened of any movement I would make to touch him. If I bumped him lightly, as if by accident, he would rush to get away. It was bad enough being on the ground; in no way would it have been safe to ride him.

In my assessment to Jill I explained, 'he is not a bad horse, he is just saying- please don't frighten me- his nerves are continually on edge anytime he is handled by people, especially strangers. When he bucks, shies or bolts with you, it is not personal. He can't help himself. Something inside switches over and he has to move. When he is calm he is a big gentle giant, but sensitive underneath. That will have been his undoing. He has been put under too much pressure too soon - to look and to ride like a performance horse. Mentally he is a wreck; physically he is poorly developed because he is under tension. His mind and body are in a downward spiral that is getting worse and the shame is it has been caused by thoughtless selfish people'.

I could see I was only confirming what Jill had already thought.

'What do we do then', she said, 'I've tried just about everything and I am rapidly losing my confidence'.

'We have to win his trust; it'll start off with small things and build up to bigger things, so that his trust will carry him through the scary times without flipping his switch. Once we have a mental connection and some understanding, he will be in a place to start his ridden training all over again. First he has to trust me, so I can get him rideable again and then he has to do it for you, because this is going to be a one person horse, certainly for the time being. What's more you have to learn to trust him as well, on top of that it is going to take time to heal his past. Are you up for it?'

'Yes', said Jill, 'if I give up now he is an expensive pet, if I sell him he's worth nothing and dangerous as well. I just couldn't do that to him'.

I spent the next week with Harry teaching him to accept me, to accept increasingly energetic movements calmly. Firstly he had to know there was a nice me, even if I was doing things that were a little scary. This started off with me stroking and soothing him; I had to be constantly aware of what my body was saying to him. If I was tense, not just in my body but in my mind he would move away. His body language would show when he trusted me - his head and neck would lower and his eye soften. I did not mind if he moved away at my touch, I quietly walked with him, keeping the rope about 3ft long, I did not want him to stand still just because I held him tight. I wanted him to stand because I did not scare him. When he finally stopped I rubbed him and then turned away to give him some peace. Sometimes I got it wrong as I stretched his limit of acceptance, and he would rush to the end of the rope in a panic. Usually this work only takes a short while until the horse will accept you touching him, moving around him, bumping into him, swinging the lead rope around his legs. The idea being he gets used to movement on and near him without feeling a need to move. However with Harry it was a long process. Even the very little I was doing was often too much and he felt he just had to move. It was different each day, but gradually he became more consistent in his response, but it took great patience.

At the same time as his trust built so did the language between us. I wanted to teach him to move for me away from my touch. Also to realise that a change in my energy, if it was directed towards him meant he should move. By being utterly black and white in asking him to move, to stop and to come he became more secure in my movements. I could get his obedience but I only knew I had his trust when he would soften in his muscles, and show no anxiety. That is why I did all this just with a halter I did not want him to feel tied up or constricted.

I would ask him to follow my feel on the rope to turn his head.

The horse follows my hand to keep the rope soft, this is not a pull. His ear pointing at me shows I have his attention.

If this movement is done equally on both sides it not only loosens his head and neck but also loosens his mental tension. The next movement is to take the bend into the rest of his body by moving his hindquarters over from the lightest of touches.

The inside hind leg moves forward and across. He is still holding a little tension, hence the tail swishing.

Other movements soon followed - moving his forehand away, backing and coming forward. Stringing these movements together we were beginning to move as one like a dancing couple. It was a little ungainly to begin with as we learned the steps. Sometimes I would lose the rhythm and flow; sometimes he would be the one to miss a step. Out of this developed the language of touch and suggestion and an increasing mutual trust in each other.

By the end of the first week he would put up with me swinging all sorts of objects near him and over him. We could move and dance around the arena. He would circle calmly at walk, trot and canter. If I strung too many movements together too quickly, and asked for too many changes of pace he would sometimes blow up. Then it was best not to insist he do what I wanted, but take the heat right out and do nothing for a while. Then I would start again with little movements, like asking him to move just one step forward and then one step back. By focusing on one particular part of his body we would become re-connected. In this way he learnt to trust me enough to accept greater demands while still remaining calm.

He has taken one step back with his near fore in response to my moving my hand and foot forward.

I could now see when he was getting near his boiling point and I tried to stay just underneath it. When I was further away from him and he was at the end of the rope he was quite lazy, so I knew his distrust came solely from close range pressure.

Jill came as often as she could to watch what I was doing and to try herself. It was difficult for her to develop awareness of what her actions were meaning to Harry, both intentionally and unintentionally. It was hard for her to control her level of energy, to be able to turn it up and down like a gas flame. At times her dance was like a car with kangaroo petrol - stop/go. It was hard for her to stay calm when he reacted violently. Slowly she won his trust and respect. But trust is a fragile thing, once lost it takes ages to rebuild and can be easily knocked again. I knew our foundation stones of trust were still very fragile. This was dramatically proved when a friend called by. I had been handling Harry for 10 days and was very pleased with his progress. I stopped to talk, holding Harry about 6ft from me, during our conversation my friend moved his hands quickly to illustrate a point and Harry's head shot up and he straight away jumped back. It had only been a small gesture, but it was from a stranger and a man at that. My reconstruction of his trust did not yet extend very far.

After two weeks I felt he was ready to ride. This may seem a long time to wait but I needed to see a change from the Harry who had first arrived. I now had a horse who was still suspicious and a bit jumpy, but not nearly so extreme. We had an understanding together up to a certain point, I knew if I pressed the wrong button his instincts would take over, which I could cope with on the ground but it would be a different matter on his back. I thought I knew him well enough not to press the wrong buttons, and if I did he would trust me long enough until I could put it right. His eye had softened during the handling and his body posture had become more relaxed, the time was now right.

Harry had worn the saddle and bridle whilst doing work on the ground: they did not bother him. All the same I decided to ride with the halter and use the rope as two reins. I reasoned that his bad experiences had been with a bit in his mouth. If I made a mistake and tweaked his mouth it might trigger a bad memory. Although I actually thought most of his problems came from what he felt the rider do on his back and not the feel in his mouth, it was best to be cautious. He responded well to the halter on the ground and would give his head in all directions to a light feel. In an emergency he was less likely to react to a strong pull on the halter than on the bit. But I did not want to even get into that situation; all my handling had been aimed at developing his confidence in me, and to understand my movements and signals. I had built up his trust, layer by layer; it just needed time to strengthen.

At this stage it was vital to progress from known steps to new ones in very small stages. So, when he would not stand to be mounted with a loose rein, I knew he was anxious. It might only be a small fidget but he was showing his feelings through that movement. I could have held him a little bit with the reins, but that would have only been tackling the symptoms not the cause of his unrest. It was essential to clear my mind of his past and adjust to what was happening before me. His body signs, however small, told me what it was like for him. If I was consistent in my body use, kept relaxed, patient, controlled my breathing and showed him calm confidence, he would do likewise. After repositioning him at the mounting block ten times, he finally started to let me stroke his quarters and his opposite flank whilst I leant over him. He fidgeted and moved when my foot went in the stirrup, not to worry just start all over again. Next I quietly sat in the saddle and deliberately made myself think, 'I don't want to go anywhere', and I waited 10 seconds quietly stroking him and then got off and did it all over again. I now proceeded doing the things I had done with him on the ground, but now from on his back - familiar actions but from a different perspective, a blend of security and progression. First stroke and soothe him so he got used to slow gently movement. Next pick up the feel on one rein and ask him to give in his head and neck and turn them slightly to one side. I rewarded his small response by immediately giving the rein back to him. This was not a pull on the rein; it was a polite request and a wait for his answer. He had given the correct answer a hundred times on the ground, his slight hesitation revealed inner anxiety. Harry's first step would be the crunch, so it has to follow on from the bend in his neck to move his quarters over. He had already given in the front half of his body, could he give in the back? I was not going to draw my leg back; I was sure any backward movements would be too much. A gradual closing of my inside leg and a drawing back of my inside seat bone and he moved over - relax and reward, do the same on the other side. His flickering ears, the slight head lift all betrayed how close to the edge he was. The first walk came out of the hindquarter yield, he was already laterally bent and soft, it only took a forward thought, a voice command and on he walked. The first movements were two circles, keeping the bend and softness and then breathe out to stop and get off. It was a good new start.

After a week he was walking, trotting, halting, and backing up. On some days he would relax sooner, he would stretch his neck down and blow gently through his nostrils; it was only after that had happened that I could ask more from him. If I tried before that, he would stiffen and tense. He did not mind the bridle, but I still kept the halter reins as well. His main worries were any sudden movement of the rider. One time I dropped the reins quickly on his neck to reward him and that sudden movement caused him to leap sideways.

He would also jump if I surprised him with my leg aid without having first gently warned him my leg was there. When he did jump, as long as I sat and did nothing it was fine. If I scrabbled at the reins he became worse. He was gradually learning to trust my body moving and it became possible to deliberately bump him. I needed to deliberately ride a little bit badly, so he would learn that these movements did not mean he had to defend himself.

At the end of two weeks I was confidently riding around the farm, where he was a lot happier than in the school. His bad experiences had probably just been in the schooling arena. His boiling point was now much further away. He could stiffen and tense at something in the trees and I knew he would manage to get through it without panicking.

It was time for Jill to ride; she prepared him with work on the ground until he was calm and receptive. I told her she would be nervous, it was understandable, to accept it and to trust in her ability to read the situation and to adapt what she did to stay in her comfort zone.

She nervously joked that she might never get on. I explained that she needed to show Harry calm confidence even when her stomach was churning inside. The way to do that is to be in control of your body movements, they must be smooth and regular with all your energy down, concentrate on your breathing, especially the out breath. It helps to make the out breath long and slow, rather like the half whistle that the old grooms used to do when brushing a horse, it has a calming effect.

It seemed to take forever for Jill to get him to stand. She would start to get a foot in the stirrup and then miss the right moment to quietly swing her leg over, so then he would move away. She stuck at it, she did not lose patience, she would just quietly start again. When she did mount she missed her balance and hung precariously on his side. My heart was in my mouth as she struggled to get in the saddle. All the days of training paid off, Harry just looked around as if to say, 'please get on with it.'

She only walked and halted, learning how to bend him and to halt just using the inside rein. In this way she was teaching him to keep soft in body and mind. Jill learnt to read those little signs that his attention was wandering, and to bring it back by giving him something to do. In this way she could begin to lead the dance again. When she got off her face lit up into a big smile of relief and joy.

Slowly Harry's confidence in her grew and so did her trust in him. Before she took him home she was quietly riding him round the farm. She now felt she and Harry had enough understanding to continue on their own. When she came back for a lesson a month later both of them had changed. Harry and Jill looked at ease with each other. She said some days he was a bit jumpy, but it was not because of what she was doing, and she knew how to handle it. To some of the other riders on her yard it seemed that she was progressing at a snail's pace. They would tell her to just get on and ride him, not to put up with such nonsense. Jill had been down that route and it hadn't worked. Without a foundation of mutual trust Harry had become a nervous wreck and was rapidly making his rider the same. What we had done was to rebuild the foundations; Jill and Harry had a mental connection and understanding. So much so that Jill found he was quite lazy at times and she had to ride him a bit stronger. Now she had a horse who would allow himself to be ridden - she could begin his training and enjoy it.

> *Help*. *But why did you not look for the steps?*
> *Christian*. *Fear followed me so hard, that I fled the next way, and fell in.*
> *Help*. *True, there are certain good and substantial steps, placed even through the very midst of this slough'*
> (The Pilgrim's Progress – John Bunyan)

They led both horses from the field; the head girl had his mare. It was no use sulking he would have to make sure it went all right today. They groomed the horses at the stable yard. Already he could see Rose was calmer under the girl's touch, she brushed and moved in such a comforting way, perhaps there was more to grooming than just getting the horse clean. His mare Daffodil seemed friendly enough; he had been able to catch her easily. As he brushed he tried less to remove every bit of grease and copied the girl's way. After a few minutes he could see Daffodil was almost purring.

The horseman was already in the corner waiting, Rose was first. She eyed the mounting block suspiciously, the girl ignored this and quietly carried on with the groundwork - walking, trotting, halting, backing and circling on the lunge. Just doing these seemed to settle her as she went through the familiar routine. He held Rose at the block while the girl talked to her and stroked her. She patted the saddle, jiggled the stirrups. Every time Rose lifted her head she lowered the intensity of the patting, jiggling, arm waving and went back to quietly stroking and soothing with her voice. Gradually Rose began to relax even with the vigorous movements. Even though the girl was making big movements she seemed to be able to do it in a calm relaxed way.

'You see she has to get used to seeing you standing and moving above her before you get on', the horseman explained.

Next the girl leant over the saddle and put her full weight on Rose's back, while he offered her some feed, Rose ate it. Now he led her forward a step or two, still eating the feed. Even while laying across her the girl did not stop stroking and quietly talking to her.

'This horse needs to be re-assured more than some, as she is so sensitive', said the horseman. It seemed no time at all and she was sitting astride, leaning forward bending low. As she quietly sat tall Rose stopped eating, so she bent forward again and soothed her.

'She won't eat if she's not relaxed, and sitting up tall and carrying your weight is always a tricky moment', said the horseman.

He led Rose forward and round in a circle back to the mounting block. Then they went through the whole procedure from the offside - no bother at all.

'That's good,' said the horseman, 'now go and get Daffodil.'

He felt a tightening in his chest. Just as he had expected, Rose had been fine with the girl. What if he failed with Daffodil as well? I'll just do the same as the girl he thought. He'd been surprised at how much noise she had made and how much she had moved her arms. He had thought you just had to be calm and quiet all the time. Also she had seemed to know when to turn it down a touch and do nothing.

She held Daffodil at the block and he started stroking her, slapping the saddle and jiggling the stirrups. Daffodil shot forward, the boy glanced quickly at the man in the corner; he still sat there impassively. As he started again the girl whispered, 'do it slowly and build gradually.' It began to go better; he could see when Daffodil tensed then he did less and stroked her until she relaxed again. Now he was feeling more confident, he realized he'd been nearly trembling and the stroking calmed him down as well as the horse. Just as he was putting his foot in the stirrup and was swinging his leg over Daffodil lifted her head and stepped sideways. His heart was in his mouth. Should he get down or carry on mounting? Before he knew it he was in the saddle and the girl had stopped and calmed the horse; she half smiled and winked at him - she had known Daffodil wasn't going to do anything. He felt happier knowing that she was going to lead the mare. He felt his resentment melt away, he now felt a bit bad about what he had thought of her. He and Daffodil seemed to click, she was not tense at all, and he felt confident that he could do this. The rest of the session went well.

The horseman seemed pleased, 'there's a lot more trust going on now', he said with almost a twinkle in his eye.

As they came out into the sunlight the girl seemed pleased, turned to him saying 'that went well didn't it?' He felt a warm glow of satisfaction; he hadn't realized how much he'd been worrying and said so to the girl.

'Now you know what it's like for the horse,' she replied.

* * * *

Trust is where it begins, but is also the middle and the end.

Each time you demand more from your horse you are testing that trust, if there is not enough go back and rebuild it.

Is it just discomfort or mistrust? It's the same for both horse and rider.

The trusting horse will follow your leadership even against his instincts.

Patience & consistency strengthen trust. The stronger the trust the more readily the horse will forgive.

The longer you take in the beginning the quicker you will reach the end.

Chapter Two

UNDERSTANDING

When your car breaks down if you know how it works it is easier to mend. If you can feel when it's not right, you can do something about it before this happens. If you know how to drive correctly, your car will run smoother and last for longer. It's the same with a horse, the more you understand what makes him tick, the easier it is to sort any difficulties or to get along even better.

There are characteristics common to all horses.

He is an herbivorous herd animal.
His survival depends on him being acutely tuned into his environment.
If threatened he will run or fight.

These facts are generally known, but each horse has an independent personality, and individual behaviour can and does vary. It is up to us to understand our horse's individual character and work out what motivates him in life, and plan our handling accordingly.

Having a horse is a two-way relationship; does your horse understand you, or just put up with you, or refuse to have anything to do with you? We have to present ourselves in a way that helps his understanding of what we require. It all sounds obvious, all just common sense, but unfortunately our feelings and emotions get in the way. We may have the knowledge but not the ability to put it across.

The guidelines to follow are: -

Observe horses in general and your own in particular.
Work with your horse's nature not against it.
First connect your minds and then your bodies will follow.
Develop your knowledge and technique.
Above all you will need to develop self-control and patience.

Some people may not want to develop a closer relationship with their horse. They may be happy with the way things are. There is nothing worse than trying to mend something that isn't broken. Many people don't have much time to put into their horses, only being able to ride at the weekends and occasionally after work. Their riding may fulfil a particular wish, maybe to ride out and enjoy physical exercise; their horse may feel the same. Such a pair already understands each other sufficiently for what they want to do. However there are others who aren't happy or who may have ambitious plans, in which case more understanding between them and their horse is needed. The next two case studies were completely different in character, but once the cause of the problem was identified the remedy became clear.

JIMMY

Jimmy was an old fashioned cob; the ride and drive sort you see tethered on the side of the road. Dawn had bought him because she wanted something steady, good in traffic with a nice nature. Jimmy was all of these, a confidence builder. He lived out, he had a field shelter, and he had company. He was fine for the first few weeks, this was the honeymoon period, and then the cracks began to appear. He was happy being ridden out in company, however when out on his own he would go so far then stop dead. Dawn had always been able to get him going again, but now the situation had deteriorated. He had started to nap and go backwards. The last straw had been when he had wrenched the reins out of her hands, turned tail and galloped back home. Fortunately she had managed to stay on and Jimmy was his old quiet self back at the farm. She let a more experienced rider take him round the farm and they had little trouble. Jimmy came for two weeks to see what I could do to help them both. Dawn was going to come three times a week because she realised it was no good just I riding Jimmy she had to do it as well. When a new horse arrives I let him settle in and get to know his personality. Just leading him out to the field on the first day told me a lot. He held his head up, looking all around. He bumped into me several times as if I was not there. Even though he was anxious he needed to learn not to invade my space. In a herd situation, even if frightened, a startled horse does not jump on top of the herd leader. Jimmy had so little regard for me that he thought nothing of flattening me. I bumped him back, on his shoulder, whereupon he promptly charged off. I let him go to the end of my long rope, braced myself, this pulled him up short and he turned and looked at me. My next move was to walk towards his hindquarters gently swinging the end of the rope, without hitting him. He moved his quarters away from this pressure and in doing so the rope came light and he stopped leaning on my hand. I then relaxed and carried on walking to the field, as if nothing had happened.

Twirling the rope to move the horse over

Jimmy and I were just establishing the ground rules. I needed to let him know not to jump on top of me. He was a strong horse and he could easily tow me down the track, so it was necessary to turn him, the easiest way was to push on his quarters rather than try and fight his head. When he moved them away he was acknowledging that I could control some of his movement. I could have asked for more submission, but the only point I wanted to make at this time was 'don't push on me'.

The next day I started his training with groundwork and soon discovered that he was both mentally and physically stiff. By this I mean that he was slow to respond to my requests to move in different directions, and when he did he would do so in a hard and braced way. I began by seeing if he was happy to stand still. Jimmy was fine with that in the school because he felt comfortable there. Next I asked him to turn his head and neck from a feel on the halter rope; he was very numb with this. To begin with I don't think he understood that he needed to follow a light feel of the rope, because apart from going in a straight line, all he had learnt in his earlier days was to only follow strong tugs on the rope. If he would lighten up his bodily response it would make his mind lighter as well. As he learnt to flex easily, first to one side and then the other, he began to soften. It is like kneading a cold lump of plasticene, to make it pliable. He would also lean on his inside foreleg and push his shoulder at me. A subtle way of showing he was not entirely happy with being re-educated. This is where the hindquarter yield is so useful. When Jimmy stepped across smoothly with his back legs, the change in his balance would unlock his tense inside front leg. The importance of this stepping over being smooth can not be over-emphasised. Gradually with this bending and stepping over Jimmy began to move lighter and more freely. He was learning that he did not automatically have to lean on the lead rope.

Some times he moved well, at others he would rebel and kick out. By consistently asking in the same way, starting very politely and only increasing the pressure little by little, then instantly rewarding his tries, his understanding of my language increased.

Basically he liked an easy life, comfort was his motivation. If his comfort was disturbed by what people did to him, or by strange surroundings, his instincts were to either fight or to run or both. My job was to convince him that there was no need to see the situation as a 'them and us' battle. Once he understood that it was more comfortable to follow my requests smoothly and lightly I could ask him for more advanced movements and patterns. When these went well he was accepting that I was the one in charge. I needed him to do this, so that he would look to me for comfort and guidance when he was away from home.

The groundwork progressed well. Together we could do straight lines, circles and lateral work. He was light in hand and his steps were becoming softer. All this was just with a rope halter. In this way he had complete freedom to find his own balance. Any form of restraint such as side reins or tack that placed him in a certain position would have defeated the purpose. It took most of the first week for him to mentally and physically develop softness and looseness. Changes of pace stretched his comfort. Trot and canter put him closer to his flight instincts.

He had arrived with a Dutch gag and a running martingale. Dawn had been told by his previous owners that this was what he needed. I changed the bit to a jointed cheek snaffle and threw away the martingale. How could I expect him to meet me halfway if I arrived armed to the hilt? I often start youngsters and horses that have bit problems with a halter, but not with Jimmy. He was a very strong horse and used to leaning on the bit. I was not going to pull at him, which would only invite him to pull back, but I did want to be able to turn him in emergency. I might be able to do that in a halter but it was unlikely that Dawn could. I needed to give her something that was effective, and within her capabilities in the time available. In retraining a horse I often have to go along with what he already knows to a certain extent, so we have a degree of connection even if it is not ideal. To ride around the farm with only a halter would be far removed from Jimmy's experience - it would either be instantly successful or a disaster. My eventual aim was to arrive at enough understanding so I could ride like that, but to begin with I needed to go along with what he knew.

The first time I rode Jimmy round the farm I went with another horse, a schoolmaster. What you feel under your backside tells you how your horse is feeling and what he is going to do next. It takes a while to learn to tune into this. Also the attitude of the head and ears tell a lot. I picked up the reins keeping them as long as possible, not tight and restricting, but not right out at the buckle, a comfortable length for us both. I rode him mainly with my body and legs, not strongly but enough to get into his rhythm. Very soon I tried him on a loose rein; he had very little natural balance and stumbled all over the place. As we were only walking I left him to sort it out. He had got so used to propping himself on the reins, now that I had taken them away it was like taking away someone's walking stick. He found it very difficult to walk downhill and generally did not know how to freely walk forward when ridden. He showed little anxiety whilst with the other horse, however when the schoolmaster trotted ahead he soon became agitated and tried to rush forward. Sliding a hand quickly down one rein and with pressure of my leg on the same side, I turned him before he could get under way. He calmed as soon as the other horse returned. At this stage he did not feel secure on his own.

After a few more days in the school I took him out unaccompanied. I thought he was accepting my guidance pretty well without showing much tension or resistance. We had only gone a little way when he gave an anxious whinny; closing my legs and giving a steadying feel on the rein seemed to re-assure him. I allowed him a toilet stop. The next second his head went down, he dropped a shoulder and set off for home. It took three or four strides to turn him, again using just one rein and leg. By allowing him to stop he thought he was in control, a classic 'give an inch and he took a mile' situation. After that I kept urging him on, just a little faster than he would have liked. When we turned for home he relaxed a little and only in the last quarter of a mile did he really lower his head and soften all over.

From this day he increasingly accepted my guidance and became more confident on his own. For Dawn it was a different matter. She needed him to stop seeing her as a passenger, but rather as a guide to trust and respect. By proving to him with the groundwork that she could control his movements and not the other way round, she had made a good start. I must emphasise that it is the manner of the control that is important. It is no use if all you do is frighten the horse by chasing him around. He has to understand your signals and respond calmly and smoothly. Certainly it won't be smooth to start with, especially if he has never been moved in this way before. But there must be an improvement, however little. Dawn learnt to look at his body to see the small signs of understanding, such as blinking, keeping an ear and eye on her, even a gentle licking and mouthing. A lowering of the head and a change in the whole body soon follows these.

Because he had got into the habit of taking little notice of her and looking after himself, she had to become more pro-active. This means giving him something to think about, which re-focuses his attention back onto her. In other words repeat the patterns and transitions that are done on the ground but now from his back. I don't mean rushing around with great energy but give him a small task to do - like stopping, turning either around the forehand or the haunches and then walking on again. As long as he feels calm do nothing, but at the first sign of a change remind him that you are there by giving him something to do. Later it will only need a closing of the legs. In this way Dawn began to be less of a passenger and more of a rider, this was what he needed to give him security. When she took Jimmy home she understood more of what he was feeling and had learnt to interpret his small body signals - which always come before the larger ones. She now knew what to do - to take charge rather than go along with his ideas. On Jimmy's part he now knew he had a rider to whom he could look for guidance when he felt insecure. His anxiety was not going to disappear, because that was his basic nature, but it was becoming manageable.

MOLLY

Molly was a typical Connemara cross; I have not yet met one that was not a bit sharp. This is part of their attraction; they make great sporting ponies for keen teenagers. Molly's problem, or rather her owner Jane's was saddling. With the correct preparation saddling a horse for the first time should present little trouble.

Molly had been saddled badly whilst being broken (I use the word deliberately as that was how it was done), she was held tightly and a saddle was forced on her back. Understandably she had exploded. After that she wanted little to do with a saddle. Molly was now at the stage where she would bite and kick at her owner as soon as she raised the saddle anywhere near. Once it was on her back doing up the girth was not much better. She was fine when it was in place; she did not mind wearing it, the problem was just the putting it on.

The starting point was to understand Molly's personality. Unlike Jimmy, her motivation was having an interesting time. She loved doing things, not necessarily in an excitable way, but she needed stimulation. She loved going for hacks, seeing new places, and meeting other horses. Schooling was all right up to a point, if what you asked her to do went along with her way of thinking. Otherwise she would turn the session around and train you to do the things she wanted. But just like a cat with a mouse she would soon get bored. Handling her was like playing chess, she could match you move for move. When she first came for schooling it took about three sessions before she began to change her attitude. She would try one evasion but if you blocked that she would not try repeating it; she would accept that you had won that move and try a different tack. At times she would become so furious that she would rear up and clap her front hooves together like a kangaroo. After three sessions she accepted that I was the one in charge and showed the nice soft side of her nature. She needed clear leadership but it needed to be stimulating. If her behaviour made you lose your temper she had won that round, because then she had a real reason to follow her instincts. You had lost her respect and what's more probably frightened her. There is a thin line between playing a game with your horse where you are both joining in, and pushing it too far thus breaking the link between you. Your horse may switch to and fro over this line at the beginning of training until an understanding is developed.

In tackling the saddling problem Jane needed to develop a connection with Molly that put their relationship on the right footing. Certainly they could be friends but only one could be the master. Over time such a relationship can become very subtle and sophisticated with considerable give and take on both sides. For the moment Molly needed to know that her owner was in charge, but in a way that was fair. Like a schoolteacher first entering an unruly classroom, first impressions and a few simple ground rules were going to be important.

Molly would come to the stable door and crowd Jane when she went in; this was a form of intimidation. Molly had to learn not to invade someone's personal space unless invited. Molly needed to be driven back from the stable door, hitting her with a stick is a crude and bullying way. It is much better to start politely and increase the pressure gradually. I asked Jane to begin by thinking that she was an important person; this was not a time to be feeling humble. She looked Molly in the eye and pictured the pony moving out of her way. When this had no effect it was time to raise the level of energy. She said the word 'back' in an imperative tone, still nothing happened. Next she swung the halter and line in her hand towards Molly, but not touching her, even this amount of energy did not move the pony. Now she flicked the lead rope at Molly's chest, gradually increasing the speed and intensity of these flicks. At last Molly flung her head up and took one step back; immediately Jane stopped all her movements thus cancelling the energy directed at the pony.

Molly stepped forward, so Jane repeated the whole process. By being persistent and patient she was teaching Molly that if she came too close things gradually became uncomfortable, but if she kept her distance she was left alone. This is a tough lesson to give, especially if your pony has been intimidating you for a long time. It requires a big change in your way of thinking and acting. Over the next week backing Molly away from the stable door became a regular discipline; just like children standing up when the teacher enters the class. Don't think that you should do this with all horses, it all depends on their personality. To act this way with an anxious timid horse would only make matters worse. For Jane this was the first step in feeling that she could control her pony's movements.

Molly did not like the tables being turned, she tried something else. Now when Jane entered the stable Molly put her head in the corner and turned her back on her. The remedy was the same. Don't feel threatened by the pony instead throw some energy against the side of the hindquarters until she moves out the way. Taking care not to stand in kicking range she flicked the end of the long rope against Molly's rump until she turned to look at her, whereupon she released the pressure and looked relaxed, welcoming and friendly. I told her to laugh and scoff at Molly when she was threatening; it is the last response the pony is expecting. Once Jane felt confident and not intimidated in the stable Molly's respect for her grew.

The same principles now needed to be applied to the saddling. The first discipline was for Molly to stand still whilst Jane stood by her side holding the saddle. Keeping a pony like Molly still by holding her tightly does not have as great a psychological effect as her standing with a loose rein. Molly was wearing a rope halter with a long lead rope that was slightly heavier than most. This meant that, if

UNDERSTANDING

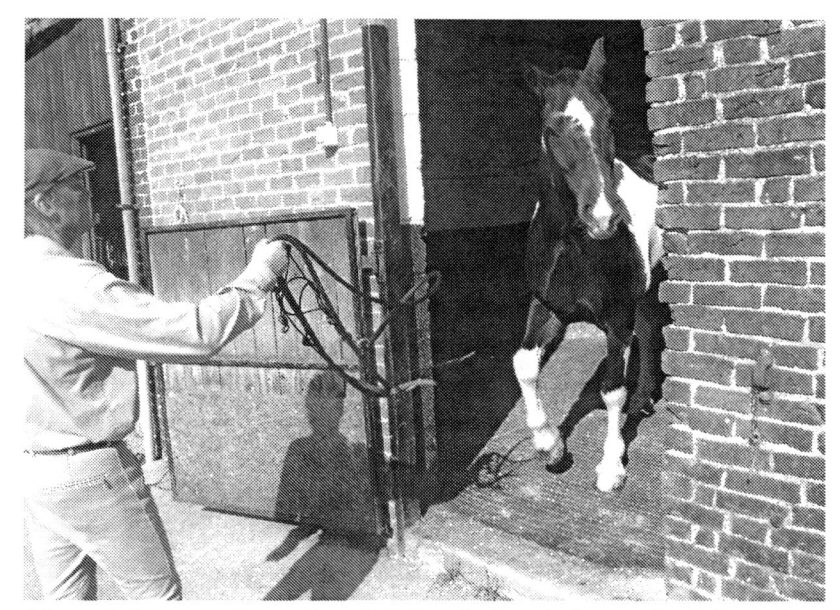

I have raised my energy by standing tall, looking the horse in the eye and swinging the halter to keep the horse in the stable.

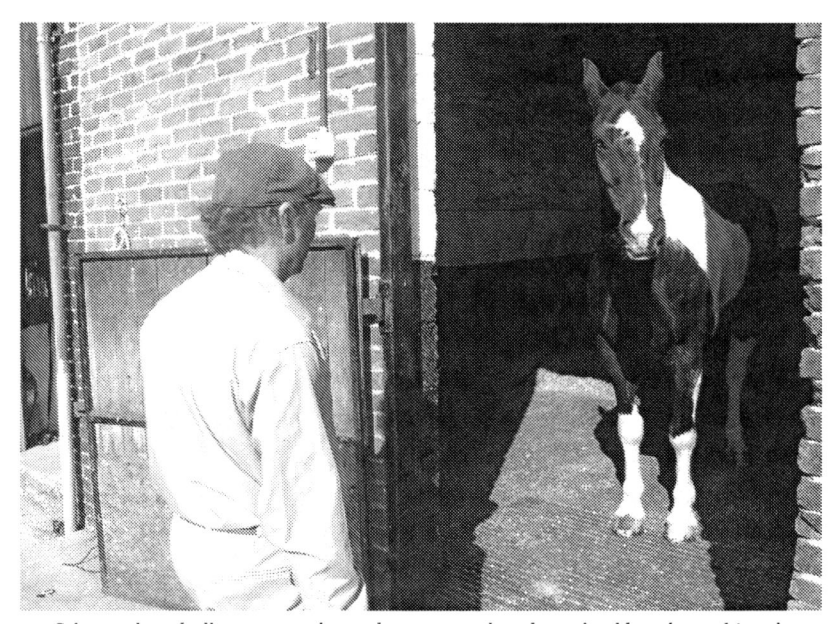

I have released all my energy, lowered my gaze, relaxed my shoulders thus taking the pressure off the horse who is now happy to stand and not threaten me.

she moved when the saddle was lifted up, the handler need only send a few quick ripples down the rope that both irritated and reprimanded. Molly tried to bite for at least six times before she accepted that she was going to be thwarted each time. Instead she began to lift her hind leg to cow kick. Jane immediately backed her up with great energy for half a dozen steps and then invited her to stand still. In this way the saddling gradually got better. Things changed from being threatened, bitten and kicked to Molly merely scowling. A problem like this is not cured over night; it was several months before saddling became normal. Even then if Jane dropped her mental guard or if Molly was in season the old behaviour would instantly reappear. The difference now was that Jane had a strategy to fall back on. She also understood more about Molly's personality and why she acted as she did. Yes, Molly had had a bad introduction to the saddle, her behaviour was partly a reflex action to being saddled and the associated past pain. Also it was an expression of her strong personality, which could intimidate Jane to perhaps give up or at least have to have somebody else help hold the pony. Jane succeeded because she followed the principles that Molly should not invade her space and that she could control her movement. Molly needed to thoroughly learn that her Jane was not to be pushed around.

> ***Hopeful.*** *And let consider again that all the law is not in the hand of Giant Despair: others, so far as I can understand, have been taken by him as well as we, and yet have escaped out of his hand.*
> (The Pilgrim's Progress – John Bunyan)

'What a stink', said the cleaner.

His room mate agreed, 'It's a mixture of the horses and that old Afghan coat of his, I never go in there if I can help it!'

Three hours earlier he had crept out of college; it was always easier getting out than in. Life at university was very cloistered, now he had found a new world - the horse world. He had been juggling both these for two months; it was tiring but so exhilarating. Once he had left the college gates at 6.30am in the dark it was like walking through the wardrobe into Narnia. Today should have been the lecture on Anglo-Saxon place names. Instead it was the 4/2d breakfast at the transport café, and then onto the farm and by 7.30am he would be riding out in the countryside. If he was lucky he could just nip back for the 11.00am lecture.

The first day this new life began had been a bit scary. He had never been to a working farm before, let alone got to know the farmer. Arthur came up trumps, it was difficult to place his age, he had that weathered look and wore an old coat that struggled to meet in the front, and on his head was a battered cloth cap. His deep rich, gravely voice licked around the words,

'You think you can ride then, ever been on any horses like these?'

It was only the twinkle in Arthur's eyes that stopped him climbing in the car and going straight back to college. He got to know that twinkle well over the next year. Reg, the farm hand was also the groom and work rider, having picked up the job over the years. It was very different from the riding school, which was all he knew. For a start the horses were much bigger, thinner and fitter. The tack was definitely more workmanlike, the saddles smaller and the leathers shorter. He had tried dropping the stirrups to his usual length but there were not enough holes! He had brought his hacking jacket but when he saw what Reg was wearing he quietly left it in the car and stuck to just his jersey. That first ride, he'd never been on a point-to-point horse before, had been a shock, everything seemed to be the opposite of what he had learnt. If he took up the reins for a contact his horse shook his head and became more excited. But if he did nothing his horse was difficult to steer and he felt helpless - it was an act of faith. Reg explained that they were racehorses off the track and were used to following each other in a string, ridden on a long rein. If you picked up on the reins they would think you wanted faster and come back to a walk when you dropped them again. In the beginning it was like driving a car with faulty controls and a mind of its own; but he soon got the hang of it. The feeling of power under the saddle was intoxicating.

The first canter had terrified him. Reg had been filling him with stories of the things that could go wrong. He was beginning to recognise when it was a wind up, but he could not always be sure. Reg and Arthur were experts at taking him in; he had been so gullible. When Reg said this was to be a half speed canter he did not know what to expect. They trotted round the 30-acre field once and they were off, he barely had time to grab at the reins and not fall back as his horse surged forward. He rammed his horse behind Reg, not giving him any daylight. He used to do this with the ponies on the beach, it had worked then. This time his horse would have none of it and pulled upsides the other horse. Reg shouted out,

'Oh, he hates being behind, forgot to tell you'.

Alongside he was easier to ride, he did not pull so much. This was the fastest he had ever been. Reg then surged ahead once more and his own horse responded to match him. The trees in the hedge flashed by, the wind whistled past his ears, he could no longer hear what Reg was shouting, just the pounding of his horse's hooves and his own laboured breathing. In no time they had done one circuit of the field. Reg stood up in the stirrups and dropped the reins and said, 'steady boy, steady', slapping his horse on the neck, who dropped to a trot and then a walk in no time at all. The student did the same and promptly fell on his horse's neck, much to Reg's amusement.

'Was that only half speed'? the student gasped!

'No that was three quarter, but it was fun wasn't it, don't tell Arthur', replied Reg.

They walked another circuit of the field; he was breathing as heavily as his horse. He had just about got it under control as they neared the farmhouse.

Arthur stepped out from behind the barn,

'That weren't half speed', he growled, 'you'll ruin their legs. Were you trying to scare the lad?' he said looking at Reg.

'I wasn't scared, I am sorry I went too fast', the student answered, fearful that he might not be allowed to ride again. 'Reg should have known better', was all Arthur said and turned away.

Now he had been riding out a month and loving it, but today was to be different. After exercising the first lot he and Reg were going to take the others hunting, to qualify for the point-to-point races. He was both excited and filled with trepidation. He knew pointers were not like full time hunters, they had to be nursed but still seen to be participating - Reg said it was an art in itself.

Yesterday he had asked Arthur and Reg what he should wear. When they said 'black tail coat and top hat' he knew by then they were just teasing him. He reckoned he could at least wear his hacking jacket and bowler and the newly bought pair of second hand black boots. He offered to come early to help plait up, but Arthur looked at Reg and said they would take care of it.

Changing from his riding out gear into his hunting clothes became a voyage of discovery. He had never been in the farmhouse before, having to turn down offers of cups of tea to rush back for lectures. In fact he had not even been in the tack room; Reg had always tacked up the horses before he arrived. The back door led into the tack room and it, in turn, led into the kitchen. At his riding school the tack room had been the holy of holies - spotless. His teacher had always told him you should judge a place by the tidiness of the tack room. He opened the door, nearly falling over a row of boots, some of which must have dated back to the war. He had entered an Aladdin's cave of farm and horse curios. There were coats of all descriptions hung on the walls, rugs stacked up from the floor, tack dangled from the ceiling, saddles jutted out, and strange slashing and chopping tools hung from hooks and nails. But it was the smell that he always remembered, a rich cocktail of leather and earth that spoke of ages past. He wound his way through to the kitchen and changed for hunting.

A little self-consciously he returned to the yard, expecting the usual teasing; Arthur and Reg were too busy to comment, adjusting breastplates and going over the horses for a last time. They saw him looking at the neat but unplaited manes.

'We aren't going to waste time plaiting them, that's just for racing and fancy folks', laughed Arthur.

The meet was in the village a couple of miles away. As they rode out he could feel his horse was more alive but controllable and a tingle of anxiety and excitement seeped through him. As they neared the village green horses were appearing from every direction, as if answering an urgent summons. He and Reg kept to the back out of everyone's way; his best clothes seemed quite ordinary, his green tweed jacket marking him out as a groom.

'Leave this to me', hissed Reg, as a smart man on an even smarter horse rode up and asked for money.

'Arthur's coming in a minute, he'll sort it out', replied Reg. The smart man rode off scowling and muttering.

'That's the secretary', said Reg. 'He's always trying to get money out of Arthur but as they go over his land he daren't be too pushy'.

They moved off, he and Reg kept to the back with the other pointers, playing a cat and mouse game, keeping up with the hunt but not getting caught up in the hurly burly of the field. He knew they had to nurse the horses until 2.00pm and avoid any jumps that might damage the horses' legs. They had been doing this successfully for two hours when a voice boomed out from the other side of the hedge,

'Come on you bloody pointers get in here and let me see you hunt, if you want to race this season'.

'That's the Major', said Reg. 'He's the master, he runs the hunt, we'll have to do as he says for a bit then slip to the back and make our way home'.

Leaving the safety of the road, jostling with the other riders in the woods made his horse change up a gear. When others were walking he was jogging, when they were trotting he was bucketing along at a canter. He dreaded to think what would happen if they came to an open grass field. He got a few sour looks when he ran up the back of the horse in front as they rode single file round the edge of the sown fields.

He was beginning to feel a bit more in control and not so scared when the hounds, which he had not seen since they moved off, began to speak. One hound caught the scent and spoke, at first just a whimper then rising to a full throated cry; this was taken up by more and more of the hounds until the whole pack filled the air like an orchestral finale. He was too far back to see what was happening, but all the horses knew; heads came up, ears pricked, riders swiftly gathered up reins. Reg shouted something about

'….. the road'. But it was too late; his horse had already decided to follow the others. Desperately he tried to slow down. He pulled hard on both reins but that only made his horse quicken. He tried to turn his head, but he might as well have been pulling at an iron door for all the good it did. Abandoning all hope he just crouched there as they galloped along. Luckily they came to a check at a small wood after a mile and when the other horses stopped, thankfully so did his. 'Takes a bit of a hold, doesn't he?' said Reg grinning from ear to ear. Never having hunted before he did not realise that the hounds did not go flat out all the time and that there were breaks when they lost the fox. This one lasted twenty minutes while the hounds went back and forth through the woods trying to pick up the scent.

The pointers stood together their riders cracking jokes about winners past and winners to come. The friendliness and camaraderie was comforting, he thought they would help him out if he had real problems. The hot horses fidgeted and moved about waiting for the hunt to start again. He and Reg were twisting around near a muddy pool when one of the lads suggested he let his horse cool his feet after the gallop. He did not think this was necessary but did as he was instructed. His horse wobbled and slowly began to collapse. Too late he realised he'd been done again. He just scrambled clear and pulled his horse up before he could roll completely. 'Sorry, I forgot to tell you, he loves to roll at the sight of a mud bath', grinned Reg. The other riders obviously knew about his horse's liking for water as they joined in the mirth. He was lucky he only had muddy boots and britches but his horse was caked on one side, any plans to remain anonymous had gone for good.

He was discovering that this stop start hunting was normal, endless galloping for mile after mile was only for books and films. They continued hacking from cover to cover with no sign of a fox, as it was nearly 2.00pm he and Reg dropped to the back and turned for home. They had not gone far when a man on the road gave a holloa. Turning, they saw a big dirty fox creeping along the bottom of the nearby hedge.

This was a revelation, it was the first fox he had ever seen, but it should have been bright red as in the books. He had little time to dwell on this conundrum as the rest of the hunt had wheeled round and were charging back towards them. Reg swore and pulled into a gateway, but he was too inept and was swept along with the tide of horses. Now being near the front seemed to revive and excite his horse even more. He was already tired, having been riding for three hours; this was not like exercising at all. A girl on a pony sped by and gave him a cheery grin. Even though the others were jumping the straggly hedges he had managed to find gaps to slip through. His arms ached, his shoulders ached, his muddy boots were slipping in the stirrups, but he clung on hoping hounds would check. To his horror they were now cantering along the edge of a disused airfield. Others were pulling up to a trot but he had no choice his horse was in charge. He dared not try to turn him on the concrete, he surely would fall but at the same time cantering on the hard could not be good for his delicate legs. Luckily he was not the only one; the girl on the pony was followed by a couple of others, but at this speed he would soon catch them up. He went round a corner like a motor bike on the wall of death, somehow his horse kept on his feet. Ahead loomed a post and rail fence on the edge of the airfield, there were no gaps, the girl on the pony pinged over, his panic rose, he was helpless. He could neither slow down nor turn. Such was his exhaustion he was not sure if he could cling onto the breast strap much longer and he was nearly onto top of the horses in front. The first one flew over, the next ploughed straight through scattering the rails like matchsticks. Following right behind, his horse galloped through the gap without checking his stride. Relief washed over him, cleansing him of his fear. The hounds had also checked, the other horses stopped and so did his. His joy was immense; he had been seconds away from disaster. He had seen himself explaining to Arthur that he had brought his horse down, lamed him or even worse. Today the Gods must be on his side.

    He spotted Reg riding up the road searching for him and made to join him before any further calamities might happen. As he left the Major shouted 'Tell Arthur its good to see his horses hunting properly'. As they walked back to the farm he asked Reg what would happen when Arthur learnt of his exploits, or perhaps he need not know. 'He'll know by the time we get back, you can't do anything in the country without somebody seeing and telling. Don't worry', replied Reg. Sure enough when they landed in the yard Arthur immediately ran his hand down his horse's front legs 'Well there's no heat in them, at least you walked back to make up for that galloping on the hard', he muttered. 'Do them up and come in, tea's ready'.

He helped Reg make the linseed and bran mashes and rubbed down the horses, rugged them up and bandaged their legs. In the kitchen he met Arthur's family. For some reason he had thought they would be just like Arthur - hewn from the soil. Instead he was welcomed by his vivacious wife and very attractive daughters. They made him give a stride by stride account of where he'd been, whom he'd talked to, and who had fallen off. He felt he failed in this as well, since he did not know the names of the woods and tracks, but that did not seem to matter; the family amicably argued with each other eventually agreeing where he had been. The hot tea, the salty bacon, the sausages and eggs tasted better than anything he had ever had before. Emboldened by the warmth of Arthur's hospitality he apologised for not being able to stop. 'You did really well', said Arthur's wife, 'the last time that horse went hunting Reg could not stop at all'. The door burst open and in came another pretty young girl, Arthur introduced his daughter called Fizz 'you were lucky with that fence weren't you', she said, then he realised here was the cheeky girl on the pony who had swept past him that afternoon.

It was his first post hunting tea in a farm kitchen, sitting next to pretty girls who accepted him as one of their family- he was in Heaven. As he drove back to college it seemed unreal, but the warm glow of aching muscles and a feeling of inner peace reminded him that it had all happened. That night when the world of academia had closed around him once more, he only had to go into his bedroom and see his muddy boots and jacket to be transported back to a friendlier world.

He could not wait to ring his riding teacher back home and tell her all about his first hunt. He was a little worried she might not approve of the informal way Arthur's yard was run or his own pathetic efforts to control his horse. He need not have worried. 'Understand this', she said, 'are the horses loved, do they look happy and well'? When he said yes, she went on, 'I've taught you the correct traditional way to give you a good grounding, but there are plenty of miserable, wretched horses, polished to death in spick and span yards. The horse's happiness must always come first; a good horseman does not always wear fancy clothes'. She laughed at his efforts with the pulling hunter and offered him a tip. 'Bridge the reins over the neck like a jockey and remember that with horses there is a time to do something and a time to do nothing'. It was many years before he really understood what she meant.

The next morning he was so stiff he could hardly move, it eased a little with the walk to the lecture rooms. He met his tutor who inquired where he had been yesterday. Apparently not many had turned up to learn about the history of Anglo-Saxon place names. On being told a minimum of knowledge was required on this subject, the young hunter turned to his tutor and replied 'I had the chance of some field work yesterday', and he reeled off the names of the three villages the hunt had passed through.

* * * *

Understanding leads to connecting in mind and body

Understand your horse's personality

Understand his likes and dislikes

Understand your own strengths and weaknesses

Chapter Three

LEADERSHIP

All herds have leaders, mostly it is one of the mares; at times of danger it is the stallion. You and your horse are a small herd of two, you must become the leader. There are many types of leaders from the charismatic to the downright brutal.

Good leadership develops and enhances: -

TRUST
UNDERSTANDING
MUTUAL RESPECT

For your horse to accept and look for your leadership you must show clarity, love and discipline.

Clarity
Horses readily understand black and white. There is little room for grey, which leads to confusion. In the wild a horse that does not conform to the rules of the herd is a danger and will be abandoned or driven out. Our intentions and communications must be given in a consistent way that does not lead to confusion. This requires *Patience and Persistence*
   Once the basic lines of communication are clear then the subtleties and nuances of the relationship will blossom.

Love and Discipline
These two go together.
Love without discipline will be ineffectual and spoil the horse.
Discipline not tempered with love will become tedious, overbearing and will destroy the horse's spirit.

Your leadership must develop **Mutual Respect**, if your love is expressed in a soft, soppy way your horse will not respect you. This is likely to lead to him ignoring you or pushing on you, nipping, biting, or even kicking. On the other hand if your leadership is harsh and cruel, either physically or mentally, you are showing little respect towards your horse. In either case you are missing out on the joy of real togetherness.

At times the pendulum will swing between love and discipline, but good leadership will require less and less discipline as the relationship deepens.

These qualities of leadership; - **mutual respect, clarity, love and discipline**
are easy to talk about, but everybody has their own idea of what they are. The following case studies show some different types of leadership.

SAM

When I visited Carol and her horse Sam, as usual I listened to how she saw the situation and then watched them together and then explained what I was seeing.

Sam was not particularly big, but he was a solid chunky cob. He was not the sort to move fast unless aroused. In a quiet way he had life sorted. Carol loved him dearly, she fed him, stabled him when necessary, groomed him, rode him out; however she felt something was missing. Most of the time he did what she wanted however at times he was strong to lead and ride. If he did not want to go somewhere he would plant his feet and refuse to move; conversely if he had an idea to go in a different direction to Carol he would quietly but determinedly walk there. She could eventually get him to do her bidding, but it took a great deal of time and effort. Carol had got used to this and thought she did not really mind, until she came to my farm and saw how soft and willingly a cob could move.

Watching them together confirmed all this. Sam had trained Carol to accept a level of performance that was nice and comfortable for him. In his own quiet way Sam was the leader. Many people have this sort of relationship with their horse, and if the owners are not bothered there is little need for change. However, now Carol did mind. Sam had dragged her to the field once too often. She had taken the first step, she wanted things to change. She now needed to take Sam back to the beginning and teach him a new language where she was the leader. Carol loved him dearly and did not want to hurt him. I told her his pride might be dented a little but we would not hurt him. In fact, when he respected her more he would soften towards her in both his mind and body. First she would have to earn his respect - it would start with small things and grow. For the horse, leadership is all about who decides what the herd does and when. This is primarily reflected in movement; when the leader moves the others follow, if the leader says 'move out of my way' the others clear a path. Carol was not young or strong, she would have to build up her confidence bit by bit.

We started in the stable with something as simple as putting on the halter. As Carol went to put it on Sam would turn his head away - he was telling her what he thought about her. If he respected her and was pleased to see her he would have come up to her. She said he did when he knew he was going out to the field; the implication then became clear to her. I suggested she view Sam like a new boy going to school. Once he has learnt the rules she could ease up. Eventually he would become like the senior boy who has considerable freedom and self-determination, because underneath he knows what is right and wrong. However he has to learn the rules in the first place.

Carol's first step was to put her hands lightly on his poll and nose and ask him to turn his head towards her. Carol had to repeat this six times before Sam would keep it turned without resistance. Carol had not realised his body language had been revealing what he thought and felt. Now she was asking him to have the courtesy to look at her. Carol asked quietly, she did not pull his head round, she let the weight of her hands and arms suggest in which direction to move his head. If he moved his head away Carol followed still keeping the touch, just putting a bit more weight in her arms. As soon as he gave she lightened her touch without removing her hands. It did not take long, repeating this request, before it became clear to Sam what was wanted; then Carol was easily able to put on the halter. In fact he lowered his head and blinked, a sign of his understanding and acceptance. Carol normally just shoved on the halter, while Sam showed her no respect and was a good as laughing at her. Now she had taken the first step in showing him she could control his movement without pulling, shouting or hitting him.

However, when leaving the stable Sam still dragged Carol after him. He might have learnt respect standing still, but he should not have moved until asked. The first rule of manners is that your horse should not push on your personal space. In a herd situation this would be perceived as a challenge, to be repelled, conceded or avoided. Carol had been conceding all the time. So she took Sam back into the stable, this time before he left the box she was going to teach him to step back. More importantly she was going to persist until he did it willingly and with little

A HORSEMAN'S PROGRESS

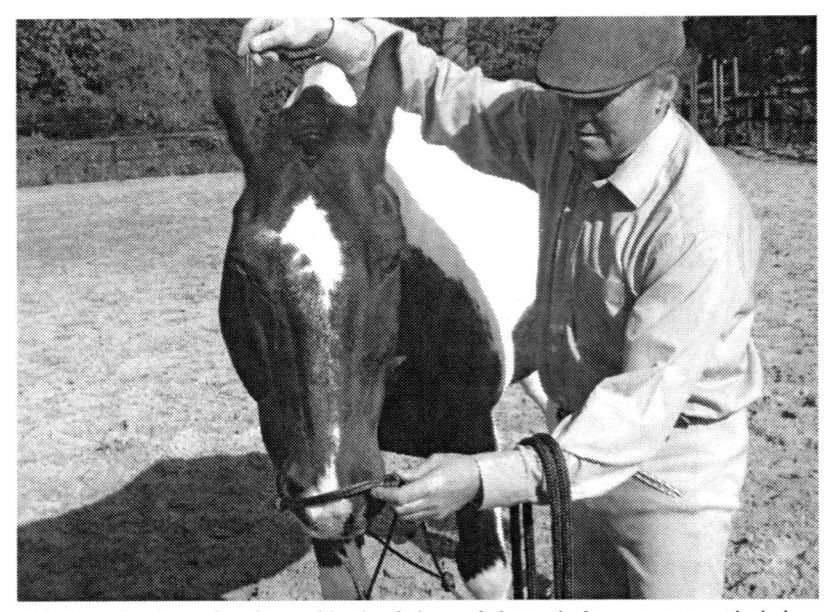

The horse has lowered and turned his head, from a light touch, for me to put on the halter.

effort on her part. This was very similar to Molly and Jane in the last chapter except Carol was going to teach Sam to understand the feel of the halter and her hand to step back. She stood in front of him, she thought herself tall, imposing and immovable (imagine you are on the edge of a cliff where a backward step would be fatal). She needed to show Sam a side of her that she usually hid. Like a sportsman psyching himself up, a dramatic change was needed if Sam was to take any notice. As Sam did not listen to the language of the feel on the halter and rope Carol needed to throw energy at him, starting mentally and becoming physical if needed. Carol, filled with inner strength and purpose, held the halter with one hand under his chin, applied a light pressure asking him to step back. Nothing happened; she applied more pressure until it felt uncomfortable for her, straining her arm. Sam still did not budge, he was quite happy to lean into the halter. Carol now swung the tail end of the rope against his chest, lightly at first increasing the rhythm and speed until it became increasingly uncomfortable. Sam tried to ignore this but he could not pretend he was not irritated, he lifted his head and rocked back. This was a start, so Carol released the pressure to reward Sam's effort; then asked again. By asking in the same way each time it soon got to where Sam stepped back from a light feel, she no longer had to swing the rope.

The horse moves back from the irritation of the energetic rope.

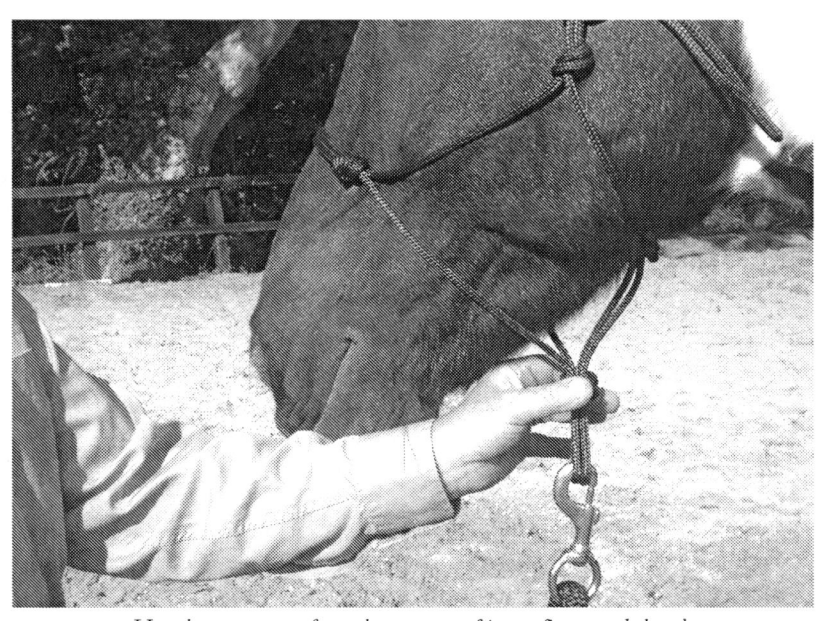

Here he now moves from the pressure of just a finger and thumb.

The two important factors for success were: -

To reward Sam's increasing obedience.
To use an effective stimulus.

Over the next few days Carol went through the basic exercises of lateral flexion, yielding the hindquarters, yielding the forequarters, back up and walk on. Some times were better than others; Carol found it hard to be consistently clear for Sam and show calm confidence. The more she worked with Sam the less she had to think about what she was doing so the more natural and confident she appeared - she was giving good guidance.

A week later Carol was having problems circling Sam at the trot. Up to now the time had been spent developing a language based on feel through the rope and the level of Carol's energy. Sam had co-operated at the halt and the walk but it was a different matter at the trot; he was kicking out at her. This upset Carol and she did not know what to do. Sam was not yet prepared to concede that Carol was in charge, so being a phlegmatic type it came easier for him to intimidate her than run away. She had been asking him to trot a circle on the end of a long rope. She asked politely, bringing up her energy and leading with the rope in the direction he should take. When he took no notice she lifted up the whip, this was not directed at him but rather behind him to drive him forward. Whereupon Sam pushed his shoulder at her and kicked in her direction. He was resenting her controlling him from a distance and asking for more speed, while she did not move at all. He did not believe he had to accept her leadership and was testing her. Carol and Sam were like two young sparring colts, seeing who would give way first. Carol had several options. She could simply hit him on the quarters and insist he went forward; after all it followed the rule to push on the part of the horse's body that was pushing on you. However Carol did not feel that she either wanted to, or could in fact carry it out successfully. Flexibility is the key to good leadership, if you are in a confrontational situation and you don't feel confident that you can readily and quickly resolve it, be prepared to alter your game plan. Maybe Carol had not asked Sam clearly enough; but on the other hand Sam knew from past experience that he could frighten her. Carol did what she felt she was able to do in those circumstances, she stopped driving him- so he stopped. Shortening the line she pulled on the rope so his head came towards her, and strongly pushed on the side of his quarters. Even this was tricky, she had to conquer her fear, feel strong and tap him with the stick on the side of his quarters until he stopped threatening her and moved them away. Because he had been so aggressive she demanded he move for several steps until his body softened. Immediately she relaxed and they both stood for a while doing nothing. A few weeks earlier she would not have noticed this change in his posture or have recognised when he was becoming tense. Now she was beginning to tune into what his body was revealing about his thoughts and feelings. Carol began again with the trot circles, it took two more attempts before he stopped resisting whereupon she rewarded him by finishing - she was the one controlling the pace and direction.

For both Carol and Sam these short sessions had represented a big shift in their relationship. She was beginning to feel more confident and less helpless. Sam was beginning to view Carol as someone of importance. The added bonus was that both of them were being stimulated by these exercises. The communication between them was growing. Carol could only progress at her speed; each small success was a brick in the pyramid of her confidence, ability and knowledge.

CASEY

Whilst Carol's story was one of establishing initial ground rules and becoming Sam's leader, Susan needed help at a higher level. Susan was vivacious, ambitious and an accomplished horsewoman. This did not mean she was satisfied with her progress; she had competed in most disciplines but really wanted to succeed in eventing. She rode a young warm blood cross, in her initial enthusiasm she had 'stuffed him up'. Casey had been lunged in side reins and ridden into a contact at too young an age, asked to carry himself like a made horse before he was capable. As a result he was shy of reaching for the bit and reluctant to go forward freely. What's more he was becoming increasingly resentful. Susan knew something was wrong and that she needed a different approach.

There was no doubt about Susan's leadership, she was in charge. Casey was well mannered, but often had a distracted far away look that frustrated Susan. It was as though he did things because he knew he had to, but his heart was not in it. I would see Casey over a period of several months. Susan went back to the beginning; she did the basic groundwork where she and Casey learnt to connect through the feel of the lead rope and a direct touch. He learnt to adjust his energy to hers, even small subtle changes. She first rode Casey in the halter, in this way he learnt to stretch and reach forward without the worry of the bit.

Horse is reaching and stretching forward on a long rein without a bit.

He learnt self-carriage on a loose rein, rediscovering his natural paces. Then he went on to accept the bit and go forward, still with a loose rein. Gradually he accepted her hand on the rein as she took up a contact. Too strong a touch would result in him ducking behind her hand and over bending.

The re-schooling appeared to be going well and Susan started to take Casey to small shows. He came to be schooled for a couple of weeks when Susan was on holiday, it was the first time I could work with him for a prolonged period and assess his progress. There was no question that he was a nice tempered horse; so why was he reluctant to go forward, occasionally resentful, and swished his tail? When Susan returned I explained how I had found Casey.

I believe most problems have a physical origin, which may become behavioural. A look at Casey's confirmation showed he had rather a long back and short weak hindquarters. His stride length and movement revealed he had greater trouble lifting his off hind. This meant he would be uncomfortable in his back until he learnt to equally swing both hind legs forward and underneath his body. This was most noticeable in his jumping. He liked to jump from speed and rarely brought his off hind through first, whatever rein he was on. It also explained his one sidedness, he could not stretch and bend equally through his back, and this was most apparent at the higher paces. Good leadership from the rider must assess why the horse is having a difficulty. Is it that he does not understand our aids? Or does he understand but physically finds it difficult? Or does he refuse to do it even though he understands? It is rare that a horse point blank refuses without a reason; it is up to us, as the rider and leader, to work out the reason. The horse can not speak but his posture, attitude and feel tell us.

Casey's problems were also accentuated by Susan's own physical asymmetries. We expect our horses to learn to balance and develop equally on both sides, so must the rider. The rider must become ambidextrous if the horse is to do the same. Susan's asymmetries were the same as Casey's. So together they went really well in one direction but not in the other. If you have ever skied or done mountaineering with a pack on your back you will have discovered that it changes the whole dynamics of movement, let alone strenuous powerful movement. Casey was having a problem learning how to move carrying a rider. Susan was not a dead weight, but a moving weight that at times helped and at times hindered.

As I explained this to Susan she was mortified. She was upset that she had been asking him to do things that were physically difficult and had even hurt him. Unaware of this she had even chastised him for not trying hard enough. Most of us do this inadvertently to a greater or lesser extent, the horse's basic nature is to be generous and he will put with a lot. When he shows his discomfort it is up to us to recognise it and work out why. Now Susan wanted to know what to do to help Casey. Back to basics was the simple answer; ride him forward, allow him to stretch, use his back and learn how to bring his hind legs through. Susan needed to think about the hind legs rather than the head and neck. I was impressed how Susan accepted this unpleasant news and wanted to put things right. For the time being the sitting trot was banned. Her legs and feel would build Casey's energy, her hands would decide which gear he engaged, her body acting as a clutch to ensure smooth engagement. Appropriate gymnastic exercises would develop his lateral flexibility, especially those that would encourage the off hind to work a little easier. However she must not work too much on the weaknesses, it is important both physically and mentally to give the horse the comfort of doing the exercises he can do well.

Susan's programme included lots of hacking over varied terrain. In this way Casey's interest would be maintained, he would be going somewhere, he would change his balance up and down hill without resentment; whereas asking for extension and collection in the riding school would seem pointless. It is always preferable to let nature work for you, not against you. In her cantering Susan made sure she was to the front of the saddle, even taking a little weight onto her stirrups, this allowed Casey's back to lift up as he brought his hind legs through.

When she returned two months later I could see the change in Casey. He had more muscle along his top line. He used to look a little wasted behind his withers but now it was filled out. Standing behind him his quarters bulged with muscle. Most of all he looked a happy horse in his eye. He still had the odd moments of resentment, but they were less. Susan was no longer so impatient, she knew she had to go at Casey's speed. The classical gymnastic exercises of transitions, circles, lateral work and changes of tempo were improving Casey's balance and ability to carry her. As he became stronger he became more confident, his movement now had an ease and softness that before was missing.

Susan's role as leader in future would be to work out why Casey behaved as he did, adjust her requests to his needs and allow it to happen in its own time. In Susan's case it was a painful discovery that her demands had been beyond his capabilities, Casey had been telling her but it took a while before she listened. Fortunately she had the strength of character to change.

Leadership takes many forms, always adjusting to what is best for you and your horse. There is no set pattern that fits all horses. Carol and Susan each needed a different type of leadership; one to be more positive, one to be less demanding.

Sometimes it is in the horse's best interest to leave him alone. A lady wrote to me for advice about a horse taken on loan. He was a big seventeen year old ex riding school horse. Though appearing sweet natured and friendly she found he was a constant tail swisher, also he would threaten to kick when brushed and having his feet picked up. He came with a reputation for being a strong ride, going on his forehand, although she was unsure what this meant.

My basic advice was to make this horse comfortable but not to dismantle his life coping mechanisms. This might sound harsh but here was an old horse that had worked all his life, allowing many different people to ride him. His tail swishing and leg lifting were expressions caused by his experiences with humans. He had built up his defences to cope with where he had been placed in life. To break down these defences would be cruel if she did not replace them with something better. As the horse was only going to be on a half loan she would have no control over a considerable portion of his life. He would still be used in the riding school and he could be taken back at any time. Certainly there may well have been stiffness and physical discomfort due to the way he was ridden. With many different people bouncing on his back he would be stiff and have little incentive to engage his quarters and to lighten his forehand. It speaks volumes for this horse's good nature that he did not refuse to work at all and go on strike. Unless this lady could be in full control of this horse's life it would be unfair to dismantle his coping mechanisms.

However she could make him as comfortable as possible. She could advance her own knowledge and education. She could make her own time with the horse interesting for him. She could be there for him if his discomfort became markedly physical and make sure the vet checked him out. She could alert the rescue authorities if he was being abused. She could help those around her to understand his and general horse behaviour.

I suggested she make friends with him. Now this does not mean forcing herself on the horse; we hate it when people try to become our best friends on little acquaintance. Rather stroke him when putting on the head collar and instead of grooming him with brushes, use her hands, doing this with feeling and sensitivity. As you stroke be really relaxed and think of your hands soothing, soaking up his tensions and filtering them through your own body into the ground and away. You will know if he likes it, he will soften in his neck and lower his head a little, he may turn and look at you, he may blink, soften his eye, and twitch his nostrils and lips. You don't have to do much of this, in fact it is better to keep the sessions short and then leave him alone. He is more likely to look forward to the next time if it is short and pleasant. For his sensitive flanks and legs it is a matter of trust. He has probably been roughly brushed by insensitive people and had his feet grabbed and held uncomfortably. He will have to learn that she is different and not going to be the same; take care and take time. She might even stroke his legs with a stick wrapped in cloth, to prepare him for her hand. Each time finishing when he is soft and relaxed even if it means back tracking and only touching him on the easy places

She will find that once he trusts her he will be very responsive to doing things that are different from his usual riding school work. She could play games with him on the ground. With either a halter and line or at liberty she could play games with poles, balls, plastic sheets, logs, the only limit is her own inventiveness. Its like stimulating children in a playgroup, you can't order a child to be friendly and interested. She could also make sure he gets turned out each day in the field with companions.

As for his riding, he is too old and set in his ways to make great alterations. When she rides him she will have to go along with what he knows and is used to. She can help him in small ways. Warm him up really slowly, allowing him to reach and stretch down. He will be like a cold piece of plasticene that has to be slowly kneaded until it is soft. As he warms up he will soften more; there will be some exercises which will be beyond him, don't try. She will know when he is struggling by his physical expression and the feeling under the saddle. He probably runs off at canter because he has had too many different people bouncing on his back and holding onto his mouth with the reins. If it is no longer the actual discomfort it will be the memory of it and the expectation of it happening again.

How she gets on will depend on much that is out of her control. So long as she does not try to change him too quickly he may learn to be bilingual. He will trust her and relax but still be defensive towards the rest of the world. Sometimes the hardest leadership is to do nothing at all.

> *'Let **Ignorance** a little while now muse*
> *On what is said, and let him not refuse*
> *Good counsel to embrace, lest he remain*
> *Still ignorant of what's the chiefest gain.'*
> (The Pilgrims Progress – John Bunyan)

The horseman had offered him Dolly; explaining that it would take time to get her going as she had had a foal, and in his experience it took at least a year for the back muscles to strengthen enough to carry a rider. He was pleased; this was his own horse he did not have to share her with anyone. He soon discovered Dolly had her own ideas. She would do so much and when she said no, nothing would make her change her mind. Dolly was over weight and unfit, so was slowly brought on with gentle lungeing followed by several weeks of just walking. Gradually trot and then canter were introduced. However it always felt as if he was pushing a rock up a hill, Dolly never flowed forward freely, he always had to drive her on. She was best out hacking, then she livened up and it was enough just to sit and do nothing.

Dolly's schooling and his education took place in the parkland. The horseman firmly believed in riding in the open countryside, making use of any slight slope. Uphill made the horse push more with the hind legs, downhill made the horse flex his joints more to effect braking. The result on the level was a more powerful longer stride. He used to measure the number of strides the horse took over a hundred yards at the trot, and then re-measure it six months later. If the training had been correct the horse would take fewer strides to cover the distance.

He spent the first month riding Dolly forward leaving her head alone, not wanting to block any impulse. He desperately wanted to fiddle with the reins to bring her nose in. He even asked the horseman about the French school of thought, which was to make the horse light in the mouth and then place the head. The reply was ' When you can achieve lightness through movement then you might have enough skill to play with the horse's mouth; leave it alone for now, you will only get confused and so will your horse.' He was not really sure what this all meant but did as he was told.

Two months later, after endless circles, transitions, changes of direction he still felt he was riding a wooden plank. He could see the horseman come out each day full of expectation and go back in disappointed. He wondered if he was asking in the right way, he still felt if he gave a few squeezes on the rein Dolly would soften to him, but it was not allowed. Then one day after a few canter transitions he trotted on a circle and felt Dolly stretch forward and soften her ribs and bend around his inside leg, her mouth felt as soft as butter in his hands. The horseman summoned him with a tap of his stick and he rode over. There was a sparkle in his eyes, 'Did you feel it, the lightness?' he asked, 'Yes,' he replied, they were both smiling now. 'That came from proper movement behind, her lightness came through her whole body, she found it herself from the position the circle placed her and the suppleness brought by the transitions and changes of direction. It's taken you two months, a skilled horseman would have achieved it in less but you needed to do it and feel it yourself. Remember that feeling!' enthused the horseman.

Over the next few weeks this softness would come and go. At times the horseman would vent his frustration, 'I've never known a breed to take as long as this to learn to move forward willingly, you can't force them, it'll come in it's own time when she's ready.' At times he thought this was wishful thinking on the horseman's part. He had tried getter stronger with his stick and using spurs but it had made no difference.

In early spring they started jumping. This began with cavaletti poles on the ground and then stacking them into jumps. Dolly jumped them all but again without flow and enthusiasm. It was at this point that the horseman became ill. He took to his bed for a few days, then rallied and came out to watch the schooling. He fervently hoped Dolly would show brilliance and enthusiasm. That day they went down a jumping lane of six fences; by the time they got to the third obstacle she was slowing down. The remaining three were a disaster, knocking them down and dropping back to a trot. The horseman went indoors disappointed. He never saw him again.

The horseman stayed in his bedroom. The head gardener suggested they ride the horses on the hallowed main lawn where they could be seen from his room, it might cheer him up. He did this for the next two days but he doubted if it gave much pleasure the way Dolly went. On the third day he returned to the jumping lane. The first time down was all right but pawky. The next time she was hesitant over the first four, then reached and accelerated for the last two. He could not believe it, so went down another time; the first was awkward then she flew the rest accelerating like a sports car. He was ecstatic - the plank could fly! He went down a third time; it was no fluke, Dolly drew into the fences and ate them up. He could feel her movement and energy beneath him. She was revelling in the joy of her own movement. It had taken months but Dolly had discovered how to move when ridden; she had to do it in her way and in her time. As the horseman said, 'You can't force them; just give them the best chance to discover it themselves.'

He trotted to the main lawn and rode around. It was the first time he felt he was being taken along instead of having to push. He hoped the man in the bedroom was watching: he thought he saw the curtain twitch.

* * * *

Horses want to follow a good leader.

Good leadership develops Trust, Understanding and Mutual Respect.

A good leader will possess Clarity, Patience, Self-Control, Discipline and Love.

Chapter Four

SYSTEMS

Anyone with a passing interest in horsemanship will be aware of different styles of training and riding - either national or individual. These are historically based; depending on the culture, needs and fashions of that time. Horsemanship, as opposed to mere riding, was an accomplishment that the nobility of Europe prized. It was part of a gentleman's education, rightly developing qualities of a moral nature as well as mere physical expertise - self-discipline, patience, compassion, leadership and judgement. Emanating from the Court of Versailles and the teachings of Gueriniere, enlightened riding spread across Europe. The pinnacle in each country being the cavalry schools, such as those in Austria, France, Germany, Sweden to name a few. Trickling downwards each country would develop its own style based on temperament, geography and breed of horse. Though often denied in today's 'global village', it is still possible to see the differences in Iberian, French, German, Italian, British, Swedish and Russian styles. This is especially so nearer grass roots level, where the exacting principles of good horsemanship have been diluted. In the competition arena the will to win often overrules the ideal.

Individual schools of thought are a reflection of the fashions and needs of the time. Hence in the U.S.A. the modern Western style was developed from the needs of the cattle ranchers and the conditions in which they worked. In Europe the fashion for the nobility to display rather an affected collected style of riding evolved into a more utilitarian one, reflecting the needs of the military. In Britain the style derived from the cavalry, the sport of foxhunting and the influence of the thoroughbred.

Throughout history there have been individuals who have exerted a major influence on schools of thought, some for good, some for bad. Horsemanship is timeless even though it is constantly being re-invented, re-packaged and presented as 'a major new breakthrough'. On a cautionary note the novice rider must beware following new schools of thought without question, without trying to understand the basic concepts.

To pick a way through the maze I can only give guidelines as to what I perceive is good and bad. It is the journey with your horse that matters, not the goal. It is important how people conduct themselves. Horsemanship is ennobling and enlightening and the best teacher is the horse himself, he is very forgiving, patient and generous. We all make mistakes, but if they aren't too big we can learn from them without doing irreparable damage to our horse. Common threads of good horsemanship worldwide can be seen where there is: -

Lightness
Fluency
Beauty
Happiness

These qualities are the same for both horse and rider. It can be seen on the racetrack, the cross-country course, the dressage arena, the trail ride, the round up, and the show jumping ring; wherever man and horse are together. There is no one way a combination must perform to demonstrate good horsemanship. Horsemanship exists in something as simple as putting on a headcollar. Don't despair, perfection is unattainable, but we can look at our relationship with our horse and have these goals in mind. Horses also have minds of their own, and often how they view us does not have anything to do with lightness, fluency, beauty or happiness. Good horsemanship is about helping the horse to discover these. I have had to accept that with certain horses I will only have an acquaintance, with others a friendship and with a very few a love affair. If I can strive for these qualities in myself my horse may let his come out. This is the spirit of horsemanship.

If one follows a particular type of horsemanship one can only interpret and execute it in a personal way. Nowadays we like to put labels on things, I would rather say I strive for good horsemanship than I followed x or y's system. The way I work with people and horses is an amalgam of all my teachers and experiences. One of my first teachers told me 'a horseman can look at a horse and know what's wrong'. I would extend my definition to 'a horseman can look at a horse and know what that horse needs.' This encompasses not just the physical but also the mental and emotional. I borrow from the traditional British cavalry school I was first exposed to. I borrow from the natural horsemanship systems of the U.S.A. and Australia. I borrow from the classical approach of the European schools. I borrow from all the horse books I have read, the teachers I have listened to, but most of all from all the horses that keep nudging me along a certain path. The following case studies show how each horse must be treated as an individual; any system must be adapted to a horse's personal needs, not the horse made to fit the system.

PADDY

Rachel was a good rider, she had great balance and she had a talented jumping pony. At home Paddy jumped fine but in competitions it was a different matter. As the jumping round progressed he would become more and more excited, bouncing on the spot and bounding over the fences. As he got more wound up he would start knocking the poles down, and go faster and faster.

The first step was to see what Paddy really thought about Rachel. Until she and Paddy were thinking and acting together in the little things there was not much hope for the big things, like a round of show jumps. I asked Rachel to lead Paddy in hand around the school. I asked her to walk quicker and then slower. Each time Paddy took a while to alter his speed to hers. When she led him around from the off side he was not so keen to march forward, and he appeared more uncomfortable.

We talked about what could be deduced from this apparently simple exercise. I explained his body language showed he was not really in tune with what Rachel was doing, it took too long for him to respond to her change of speed. There was nothing wrong with this, he just did not realise that Rachel wanted anything better, and Rachel did not know that it could be better. Also she had not noticed that he was more uncomfortable when she was on his offside, she just thought he was being more stubborn. I pointed out how Paddy's eyes were set on the side of his head, unlike us who have our eyes close together on the front. This means we see in binocular vision, both eyes focussing together on what we look at. Whereas the horse can only see with both eyes when looking directly in front: he will lower his head to look at close objects and raise it to look into the distance. So when Rachel was by Paddy's side he could only see her with one eye; this was fine on the left side because he was used to her there. However it made him anxious when he could only see her in his right eye on the off side. This was because about 90% of his experiences with humans on the ground would have been in his left eye. Most people lead from the left, headcollars are made to go on from the left, rugs do up on the left, and most times we mount from the left side. The right side is more of a blank sheet, which is both good and bad. It means your horse is initially more wary on that side, but he won't have been tarnished by bad experiences. Generally Paddy looked out for himself first and thought about Rachel later. She had not realised the cause of his behaviour but now she would be able to try to help him to accept her on this side. She said it was better when she was riding.

Rachel showed me his walk, trot and canter. In walk Paddy was relaxed and calm in his body. In trot he went a little too fast, his rhythm did not look pleasing to the eye. Sensing this Rachel shortened her reins; he slowed but turned his head to the outside and leant on her hands. When she asked for canter, she shortened her reins again, he tucked his nose in and struck off with a little hump of his back and a swish of his tail. She said he always did that.

It's difficult to explain something that seems obvious to you but not to someone who does not think along the same lines. I know that when I first realised what my horses had been telling me over the years, I felt so guilty. Understanding is the first step towards reconciliation; try to see it from the horse's point of view. Paddy was happy at walk, at trot the increase in energy made him anxious so he hurried. Then when Rachel picked up on the reins, he knew he had to slow down but felt tense, so he leant on her hands and braced his body looking to the outside. At the canter these minor symptoms were magnified. He dutifully tucked in his nose when the reins were shortened for the canter transition. He felt the surge of energy asking for the canter but he could not stretch his head out, so the only thing left was for him to show his discomfort by lifting his back and swishing his tail.

I wanted to get them both more connected. At the moment they were like two disco dancers, each following the music but not dancing together. If Rachel and Paddy made more of a mental connection and tuned into each other, he would be more likely to listen to her in the jumping arena rather than look out for himself.

She went back to leading him around the arena. This time when Rachel walked forward, if Paddy did not step forward at the same time, she would tap him with her hand on his back until he did. If he did not stop when she stopped, she would take and release on the rope until he did. It took at least half a dozen transitions before they both came into step. Now they were beginning to dance together. Having made an initial connection it could be developed with more complicated steps. Whilst walking round the school Rachel asked Paddy not only to speed up, slow down and stop, but walk backwards with her. To begin with she had to lift the rope for him to understand backwards, but soon he was following just her body movements and level of energy without the rope being used at all.

I wanted Rachel to feel Paddy's natural rhythm at the trot. She rode a circle at the trot with a loose rein, when he hurried I suggested that she made corrections with just one rein at a time, releasing it in between corrections. This was strange for her to have nothing to hold onto and equally strange for Paddy to have nothing to lean on. Rachel also had to feel really relaxed and not let his excess energy make her feel energetic as well. Instead of her following his feeling I wanted him to pick up on her feeling of calm and slowness. Often just controlling the breathing with a long slow outbreath is enough to release the tension in a rider's body. It took at least ten circles before Paddy slowed his trot, lowered his head and quietly blew through his nose. I asked Rachel to notice these signs, and remember how Paddy felt under her when he relaxed; she could build up a library of feelings for future reference. She gradually brought him back to the walk, using the inside rein and leg so he spiralled down into the transition, nice and smoothly.

Next was the canter, she was to ask for the transition on a long rein. Paddy was not mentally ready to strike off with his nose tucked in, that would come later when he was soft. Rachel had never asked in this way before, always being told to take up a contact. Paddy needed to become happy cantering unhindered, after that Rachel could think about a contact.

Rachel and Paddy went away and practised the groundwork and the loose rein riding for a couple of weeks, after which they were beginning to listen to each other. As for the jumping, it was necessary for Paddy not to be made anxious by being held together. He had the energy in the show ring, but it must not be so much that he stopped thinking about the job. If Rachel could learn not to hold on or fight him, but practice changes of pace in between the fences Paddy would begin to listen. This was something to set up as a training exercise. Since Paddy only became excited away from home we took him to a nearby cross-country course, which should provide enough stimulation. I asked Rachel to remove the running martingale. The rider often feels safer with this on but it makes the horse feel even more contained and held down, thus exacerbating the problem. The head and neck are the horse's balancing arm, especially so in jumping. If he is given freedom in his head and neck he will gather himself up, stretch out, lift his head as he feels fit, in order to keep himself instinctively balanced. Preventing this is like running up and down hill without using our arms; it is possible but requires much greater effort.

Jumping is all about keeping a balance and a steady rhythm. When the rhythm is lost it should be re-established quickly, as smoothly as possible and then the horse left alone. Rachel first practised this on the flat. In nature when a horse slows down he does it in two ways: either he lifts his head and lowers his quarters or he jumps his quarters sideways. If you watch horses playing in the fields you will see different combinations of these. In effect the driving and propelling action of the engine, the hindquarters, has to be checked; this is done by collecting the energy underneath and braking, or by throwing it out of gear sideways. Since Paddy did not listen to Rachel's hand when he was excited it was better to control his pace with unilateral aids, using a hand and leg on the same side. Trotting around the practice jumps was enough to stimulate Paddy, so rather than tug on both reins as soon as he sped up Rachel applied the left leg behind the girth and turned his head to the left with her hand. Her other leg and hand just allowed the movement. This is best executed with the horse in a jointed bit as it allows a unilateral action whereas a straight bit will also affect the other side of the mouth. I asked Rachel to think of this mantra: -

Engage Brain
Engage Body
Engage Legs
Engage Hand

It should be in that order even if the whole sequence only takes a fraction of a second.

Bending the horse to stop using just the inside leg and hand.

Think what you want - to stop
Use your body - stop following the forward motion and relax
Use your leg - yield the hindquarters
Use your hand - turn the head and neck

The first time was rather clumsy but successful; once Paddy had stopped, Rachel gave the rein and invited Paddy to stand still. The better Rachel's timing and smoothness the better Paddy stopped and felt happy standing. The aim was that Paddy would begin to accept that Rachel could control his pace without him becoming too agitated. The important part was that there was something in it for the horse - a reward. In this case it came from the release of the rein and leg aid immediately Paddy came to a stop.

The schooling continued over several weeks, at all three paces, until the pair was listening to each other. Rachel learnt to do something before matters got out of hand, she was showing leadership. Paddy was learning to listen and accept this guidance. Obviously it was not practical for Rachel to go round a jumping course bending her horse all the time. But by now there was enough understanding that Paddy would respond a little to Rachel's feeling of slowing and a much more gentle rein aid would tidy it up. Now was the time to begin to use both reins. However one rein would be passive and holding, the other would be intermittently active with lots of give in between. This is simply a strong half halt repeated on one rein, it is not a constant pull. If it has to be so strong that you are pulling the horse sideways it is necessary to go back to the earlier training of bending stopping and waiting. Again it took a while before Rachel learnt not to tug with both reins. In fact when Paddy accelerated she held her nerve and did nothing, following his movements without interference, then circling and positively asking for a stop. The difference, now that she was using both reins, was that Paddy was tolerating a feel on both sides of his mouth. It was a long process; it was something that had to be learnt by both of them. The aim was not to kill Paddy's impulsion and energy, just to control and guide it and keep him listening. Ponies are very quick witted and so long as they don't become over anxious and are blindly running away, it is best to leave a pony like Paddy to decide about how to jump the fence. It was only when he 'lost it' that he stopped making sensible decisions. Rachel's job was to keep the rhythm and fluency that was comforting for Paddy.

It took three months before the results were seen in the ring. Paddy began to get placed in competitions with the occasional win. More importantly Rachel felt that she could control his speed when necessary and not become frozen, holding on at faster speeds. She also discovered that after each competition it needed at least three days of schooling and re-connecting to fine-tune their understanding. It is the same with musicians, they have to re-tune their instruments after a concert. Whatever Rachel had learnt about jumping she needed to adapt to her pony's individual needs. Once she had understood why he acted the way he did she could make the necessary changes.

I dislike it when people say 'I do dressage' or 'I have a dressage horse'. I like Henry Wynmalen's definition of dressage - 'taking the horse beyond the stage of mere usefulness'. Unfortunately many dressage horses never even reach the stage of usefulness. However it does take courage to appear in public and invite other people to judge you and your horse. The very fact of entering a competition increases the desire to win and sometimes the goal of harmony disappears.

Most horse training books mention that the horse needs to be calm and his mental state is important, this is usually in the first chapter. The rest of the book will be devoted to the techniques of riding and training with little further reference to the horse's mind or how he reflects his feelings. I am sure the authors were well aware of this non-physical side of things, but the fact that it is mentioned so little means that the reader may not realise its significance. Is the horse calm, does he trust the rider, does he understand the language of the aids, and does he appear to be happy? Without these qualities the resulting physical performance is meaningless. If the rider is lucky their instructor will recognise what their horse is telling them and address the problem. More often than not the horse will be rushed through the initial training, so physically he gives the right appearance. A closer look will show that he lacks that calm enjoyment and togetherness of a horse that is psychologically sound. This lack of emotional and physical harmony can be seen in child sports prodigies who are pushed too hard too young, like some gymnasts and tennis players; they end up burnt out having missed out on their childhood.

DOMINO

Anne was an experienced competition rider who had reached a high level but she felt some dissatisfaction with her achievements. She felt she was lacking lightness, fluency and was worried whether her horse was enjoying their time together. Her horse, Domino, lacked both mental and physical balance. With some horses of poor confirmation lack of balance with a rider is purely physical, in these cases time and correct training will help. Domino had good conformation but he had lost the forward urge and stretch in his body, he showed reluctance that disappointed his rider. She did not want to compete with a horse that did not like his work.

Basic riding consists of producing a willing horse that goes forward from light aids, stops and turns easily. If your horse is left alone to find his balance as a youngster, ridden on a long rein, it will take six months to a year for a four-year-old to develop the muscle along his back to carry the rider easily. This was the old way. A horse was backed as a three-year-old, turned away then brought back as a four year old and lightly ridden. Real work did not begin until five and at six the horse could be considered produced but still referred to as a young horse. Following this system more years would be put on the horse's working life. Now due to pressures of time, finance and the belief that our horses have better conformation today, few people take this time. Despite better breeding not all horses can mentally go this fast; those that do are often prematurely burnt out.

Domino was one who had been asked do too much and quite sensibly he was saying 'I am not ready'. Fortunately he had not gone far down this route. Anne understood the whole horse must be catered for: he had turn out, companions, he was happy in everything except when being schooled. As soon as Anne asked for a contact (a much-abused term of description) he would slow and come behind the hand to avoid the feel of the bit. Instead of allowing the horse to learn a natural balance with the rider, it is tempting to speed up the process by compressing the spring.

This means asking the horse to produce energy behind and receiving it on the hands; in this way the horse's hind legs carry his and the rider's weight rather than just propel it forwards. The hind legs will give the feeling that he is lifting his back and he will stretch his top line of muscles from the tail to the poll at the top of his head. Thus strengthening his back and lightening the weight on his front legs. In theory it is understandable, in practice it takes time and skill to achieve and only comes after the horse has developed a natural ease and balance with a rider.

In Anne's case the answer was to go back to basics and teach Domino to understand hand and leg actions separately. Baucher, the French horseman who had a great influence in the C19th, coined the phrase ' Hands without legs, legs without hands'. This means do not push on the accelerator while standing on the brakes. The horse can not understand what you mean; he has to learn the hand and leg aids

The horse is ducking behind my hand and ignoring my nagging legs.

separately. Other schools of thought say one has to ride the whole horse not just one end at a time. This is very conflicting and confusing advice for the beginner; of course both schools are right, but expressing a mutual aim with different words and images. Anyone who has backed a horse will know that when you first squeeze your legs, nothing happens. Why should it? Your leg pressure is not very different from that of the girth, which you have just spent days, teaching him to ignore. Your horse learns a squeeze means go forward from how he perceives your feel, your energy and your reward when he hits on the right answer. It is the same with your hand; he has to learn to give to the feel of your hand on the rein. It helps if the hand action is taught from the ground, before you sit on his back. Going forward from the leg is a learned response, which also has to be taught. Both hand and leg aids are sometimes taught cruelly and quickly with severe bits and whips and spurs. In these cases the mental co-operation is missing; it can be done a better way with understanding on both sides.

Once your horse understands to go forward at a certain pace he next learns to stay at that energy, that speed without you having to continually ask him. He stays there by your thought, the feel of your body, which says ' let's keep going'. It is the same with the action of one leg, asking the horse to yield sideways. The first touch initiates the movement and then breathes in time with each subsequent step.

Likewise a hand action will ask the horse to alter speed or balance, then its action ceases and allows the horse to become comfortable. In other words each leg and hand aid asks, elicits the required response and then ceases. So one does ride the whole horse all the time, your body is the co-ordinator between hand and leg, yet there is enough distinction between the signals for the horse to understand what is wanted. To start the distinction is very clear and gradually the signals are brought closer together. The subtleties of riding and communication have to be learnt. Think of the time gap between a child learning the alphabet and the same person holding an erudite discussion; apart from a few infant prodigies it is considerable.

Anne's problem was her legs were continually saying 'go', but Domino was not responding. As with people if there is continual nagging, after a while you take no notice. By now Domino had what I call an emotional problem with the bit, he was confused and not confident with it, hence his excessive chewing and overbending. I believe riding without a bit; using a halter or a hackamore without metal cheeks can be a useful tool. It is a stepping stone towards a bridle. Anne used the halter and rope reins to relearn how to use her legs and for Domino to learn how to go forward freely. This was a difficult discipline for Anne to accomplish. I told her to imagine her legs were pressing a button on the horse's side. As with a button a certain pressure activates it, more pressure does not bring anything extra; it's just a waste of energy. If the button does not work you have to repair the connection. For Anne to repair the connection she needed to bring up more energy. The sequence was this; first think forward, look where she wanted to go with purpose and then give a gentle squeeze with the legs just behind the girth. If nothing happens your horse needs to feel more energy to move. For some people this would be a whack on the backside, but maybe just stimulation is better than pain. If we look at nature, horses give each other warnings and stimulation before they kick or bite, so why not us? If I am riding a young horse for the first time who does not respond to a squeeze, it is usually enough to slap my own thigh a few times for him to feel startled enough to move. His reward is that I cease the slapping, stroke him, tell him has done the right thing and most important stop squeezing with my legs. A young horse is a 'carte blanche'; he soon picks up my feel and intention. So long as I follow the same procedure, refuse to allow myself to enter into a squeezing match, he soon learns to move from light leg pressure. An older horse like Domino is a different proposition, he had become insensitive so he needed more stimulation. Anne had to slap him first on his side, then repeatedly on his rump. The key is that this stimulation is graduated in intensity, first light slaps that the horse hardly notices but then they become harder and quicker. Instead of your hand you could use a short piece of rope or a short stick. The trouble with a stick is that many horses are resentful or fearful or choose to ignore it and put up with the pain. This is especially so if a thin cutting stick like a twangy dressage whip is used without judgement and control. The key is to increase the stimulation gradually and cease as soon as the horse tries for you.

My legs have given a light squeeze re-inforced with a swinging rope, the horse has jumped forward and I make sure my hand gives the rein – opening the front door.

Anne found it difficult to follow this sequence. She would use her legs too strongly, and for too long before she backed them up with an increase in energy. By dint of telling her that I could see her legs move she gradually acquired the necessary self-control. Anne was riding with the halter on a loose rein so Domino had no reason to feel he was being prevented from going forward. It is impossible to say too often - if the horse does not go freely forward from light leg pressure the rest of the training will fail. When he did respond she made sure he did not go very far and stopped him before it became his idea to stop. In this way his energy and his co-operation were both built up; he learnt to keep going without Anne nagging with her legs. Over a period of a few days the length of time he kept his forward impulse increased. With a horse like Domino it is really important to keep his interest and always end the session sooner rather than later.

Teaching Domino to accept her hand without losing the forward impulsion was harder. Anne started by riding on the halter with a loose rein, then picking up a long rein. Even this was enough to slightly check his stride; repeatedly picking up the reins and dropping them accustomed him to a long rein while maintaining the forward urge. She soon found he went lighter, being more responsive in the halter than the bridle because he was not anticipating the hand on his mouth and thus chewing or backing off. To teach him to slow or stop it was just necessary to have a very brief hand action; a take and give repeated in intensity until he responded. This starts as a brief drag on the rein, a very gentle closing of the fist and opening again; at its greatest it is a strong take and release, like a quick electric shock. Initially this would be done in a forward and upward direction. If this fails, because you would not want to be doing this all the time, the next step would be to yield the horse's hindquarters and turn the head to spiral down to a halt. If the pressure has to be more than what feels mildly uncomfortable for you, the repeated upward and release action will ensure the horse has nothing to lean on. It lifts up his head and neck thus shifting more weight onto his hindquarters, and gets the rider out of the habit of pulling backwards. This is a teaching sequence, once the horse understands and obeys your hand action such exaggerated movement won't be necessary. I should stress that this is done with the halter, which is more forgiving for the horse. Anne put this into practice and after several tries Domino was accepting her hand and slowing or stopping without over bending. Not only was she separating leg and hand movement she was making sure her body was not telling the horse something different. In other words she would breathe out and relax when slowing, taking her energy right down: whereas to go forward she would bring her energy up.

The halter had prepared Domino for re-introducing the bridle. I told Anne it did not matter where Domino put his head, so long as he accepted her hand on the end of the rein. Gradually he became more consistent in going forward whilst she had a feel on the rein. Now that Anne had, in her mind, separated leg and hand action she was able to bring the two closer together without Domino losing his forward urge. From this basic understanding she could proceed to think about the whole horse.

The point I want make is that Anne knew she needed to balance Domino between hand and leg but did not know why it was not working. The training manual or the riding instructor might tell you what to do, but if this does not work the rider has to break the difficulty down into its basic parts, see which one is not understood by the horse, repair that and build up again. At the same time the rider has to learn the mental and bodily self-control, so as to always ask the horse in a clear and consistent way. It takes time but it is a great learning adventure. That is why horsemanship was considered an essential quality of a Gentleman.

> FAITHFUL. *Well, I see that saying and doing are two things, and hereafter I shall better observe this distinction.*
> (The Pilgrim's Progress - John Bunyan)

He had spent the summer in the Alps, he was fit and tanned, he did not carry an ounce of spare flesh. To borrow a quote from Scott of the Antarctic, his mountaineering had been 'a physical expression of an intellectual passion'. Ennui lay heavily on his shoulders. With the intolerance and selfishness of youth he was making heavy weather of this family holiday; the Emerald Isle had yet to sparkle for him. When he was not sightseeing he devoured books; humanism, existentialism, he knew about them all. One wet afternoon found him in yet another bookshop, this time in Cork; last week it was Waterford. Scarcely knowing how, he was standing in the 'Sport and Hobbies' section; minutes later he walked out with a copy of Colonel Podhajsky's 'My Horses My Teachers'. Some of life's crossroads are small and not well marked only assuming importance from a greater distance. In this book was a different 'physical expression of an intellectual passion', perhaps less expansive but equally captivating and inspiring. At harmony with Nature, it was the same thing; the journey being more important than the summit, which could only be transitory. The spark had been struck.

It was the smell, which was intoxicating, row upon row of books, shelf after shelf, room after room. The Victorian vicarage reeked of learning, of lives and experiences distilled between the covers. Every book was about horses and horsemanship. Not just half a dozen in the sports section but thousands. He had never heard of an antiquarian horse book specialist. This man was a jewel, his home was a gem, and his books sparkled. Where to begin? It was like stepping into the biggest sweet shop ever, given a bag and told to help yourself.

On that first visit, yes there were to be many more, he brought back a Goldschmidt and an Astley. The more he read the more his appetite grew, he never came away with less than two books. He discovered Baucher, Steinbrecht, Rarey, Mctaggart, L'Hotte, Fillis and many more. The cross-references were so many he began to see these old masters as friends. All the books led back to one man

Francois Roubichon Gueriniere and his book 'Ecole de Cavaliere'. He had seen these brown leather bound books with gilt banding and knew they were out of his league. They were on a separate shelf, above the others. Only on his fifth visit did he dare ask the guardian for a look; he felt he needed to show his commitment as a serious scholar, a refusal would be too hard to bear. There was an original Newcastle, several veterinary treatises and there nestled in the corner a small Gueriniere. It was in French, he could not read French, it cost far more than he could afford, but he had to have it; he had known that as soon as his eyes had strayed to that shelf.

Back in his room at college, he could see it on the shelf and feel a warm glow inside. Here was the father of classical horsemanship just six feet away. At his fingertips the map to the future: it took many years to read the map.

The more he read the less he knew. One author said one thing, another said differently; both sounded logical, which was right? In some eyes the Duke of Newcastle was a brute, in others he was the inspiration for Gueriniere. Baucher was a genius and an innovator to many and a pathetic parody of a horseman to others. Chamberlin saw no need for collection, Littauer the same, the Italians had the forward seat, Berger dismissed the natural way - it was a mass of contradictions. What was the difference between the Romantic and Teutonic style? All he could conclude was that each author thought his way was the best. Were these writers advocating genuine truths or trying to make a name by criticising others?

As his collection grew he was able to discern patterns. There were straight technical books, which he found heavy reading. He would lose interest when the book went into detailed sequences of aids to perform certain movements. These writers appeared to treat the horse as a machine - press the buttons in the right order and the movement happened. When he tried it he could not remember the sequence and his horse definitely had not read the book. There were anecdotal stories like Black Beauty, Old Sport and Horse Lovers. He relished these, even though they were sentimental, because the heart was in the right place. Some books he did not like, it was hard to pinpoint why but at the end he felt the horse had been demeaned or exploited. He realised that over the last 250 years many authors had tried to say the same thing. However each expressed it in the language, the idiom of his time. So when Podhajsky spoke of self-control, discipline and patience his words were those of a proud officer of the Austro-Hungarian Empire. Baucher's words were those of a man not from the ruling classes, a man with something to prove. People in authority, or from the cavalry wrote most books until the late C20th. They were used to wielding power and had servants to look after their horses. Their characters were moulded by the society they were raised in and it was reflected in their writing. What their horses were asked to do and the way they went were determined by the era and its fashions.

The student built up a sizeable library. Some books he only partly read, he either could not understand them or he did not warm to the author's ideas. Years later, as his experience and understanding grew, he would pick up a book and realise he knew what the author had been trying to say. Podhajsky had fired his enthusiasm because of his love for his horses, how each was treated as an individual. He had two favourite books - 'The Reforming of Dangerous and Useless Horses', by Lieutenant Mike Rimington and 'Outdoor and High School', by Captain E. Beudant. Two very contrasting books but with a common thread of care and understanding.

Beudant's book fascinated him because of its contrasts. It gave a glimmer of how to achieve that elusive harmony. It said enough to bewitch but still left it a mystery. Such sentences as 'obtain lightness, put the horse in position, and add impulsion, is all you need', said so much and so little. Yet this man obviously thought about the horse's nature and worked with it, not against it. Again further contrasts; he would extol the virtues of riding across country on a completely loose rein, then a few pages later he could be seen cantering backwards with the horse on three legs. One seemed the ideal the other the height of artificiality. Yet in both there was a harmony and his horses did not look unhappy. Little glimpses of the man's character would peak through. He was obviously proud of his undoubted talent, but wrote with a feigned self-deprecation in high blown flowery language. This would be expected of the French officer class in the early 1900's. He was proud to serve France but bitter at being posted to Morocco. Then the book was a translation from French into English by an American cavalry officer Lt. Col. John A. Barry. The book was filled with photos of American show jumpers, yet the text hardly mentions jumping - yet more delightful conundrums. Beudant did not have the full use of his legs after an accident, but claimed he rode even better and achieved even more lightness. Curiously this paralleled the latter end of Baucher's career; after his own accident he advocated even more lightness. The student took this point up with his teacher, 'Why do we have to be old and nearly infirm before we become horsemen, when it's all written down by past masters? Aren't they trying to save us years by passing on their knowledge?' She replied ' It does not work that way, you have to experience these things yourself, make your mistakes and learn from them, only time makes a truly great horseman'.

Rimington specialised in retraining dangerous horses for the army at the beginning of the C20th. There were photos of him riding buckers, rearers and bolters, all the retraining done without cruelty. This was a book of both horse psychology and practicality; there was even a chapter on teaching you how to deliberately fall off. This book captivated the student, he hoped he would never have any horses like these, but if he did, he could see all was not lost. Rimington did not just retrain these horses for experienced riders; they went back into regular service for the ordinary troopers to ride. The explanations of why these horses acted as they did, and how to use horse psychology to turn them round, instead of tying them up and tiring them out, opened a new door in the student's learning.

Looking at his books the student felt depressed; the more he read the more there seemed to be to learn and the less he knew. He asked the horseman about this, who replied,

'You never stop learning, these books are snapshots of what these authors think at that particular time. They might think differently a few years later. I have been asked to write a book, but how could I, I am still learning?'

After the horseman had passed on, the student packed his bags and prepared to continue his journey. Just before he left he was given a book from the horseman's library. It was a signed copy of 'Equitation' with a personal message from the author Henry Wynmalen. He would always treasure this book, not just for what it said but for the help the horseman had given him in pursuing his intellectual passion.

* * * *

Any system of horsemanship must strive for:-

Lightness, Fluency, Beauty, Happiness.

Rarely can the ends justify the means

Chapter Five

BALANCING THE BODIES

This chapter is about the rider's seat or how to sit on a horse. There have been many books devoted to this subject; the importance of a good position on a horse is universally recognised. It is the single most important factor affecting how the horse goes. It does not matter how much you might know about training if your horse is not at ease carrying you.

As a student I was obsessed with my riding position. I would get the book out, study the pictures, sit astride a chair and look in the mirror to see if I had got it right. I was a perfect classical chair rider but far from it on horseback; the difference being the horse's motion. A good position undoubtedly helps your horse but often we see very successful riders competing in all spheres who do not appear outwardly to conform to the ideal. What is it that they have got that elicits the best from their horse?

Flow
Balance
Togetherness

They are at one with their horse in motion, going with his movement without disturbing the horse's balance. They have a surety in the saddle that allows them to give their horse clearly identifiable signals.

The ideal seat alters according to what your horse is doing. The jockey on a race horse, the dressage rider and the show jumper are all helping their horse each in a different position. Put simply their balance is following the horse's balance whether it be upwards in piaffe, stretched out in gallop or basculed in jumping. It is important to remember riding is a moving flowing sport. First it is necessary to acquire stillness, a melting into the horse. This comes from releasing and lengthening. We should ride with our bones; the joints absorb the horse's motion. It is the muscles that hold these joints tight, learn to release the muscles and the joints will become more open and supple. Learn to lengthen the released muscles and the rider can stretch with tone not tension. It is the lower torso that first needs stability, beginning with the seat bones; the upper and lower bodies reach away from this area. Get the middle bit right and the rest will follow. Riding a horse is like a surfer riding a wave; once you and your horse are moving as one then you can tidy up the details.

Having achieved this connection between your body and your horse's, being plugged in as it were, you can use your balance to assist and alter your horse's balance. Good riding has nothing to do with tensing, bracing or holding; it is accompanying and leading. Your balance can lead your horse into the half-pass, the canter transition, and the gathering stride before a jump: where you go your horse will follow.

Good riders can feel the horse's rhythm and go with it. The horse in turn will feel any changes in the rider's rhythm and follow them. That is how a good seat blends the sometimes conflicting signals of hands and legs; it is the rider's trump card.

PHILLIP

As a child I used to ride the ponies back to the field bareback. Sometimes I slid off, sometimes I fell off but I learnt how to stay on. My sister and I never dared tell the riding school proprietor that we had fallen off, because we weren't supposed to be riding them in the first place! Riding bareback or being lunged without reins or stirrups is the quickest and most effective way to learn to sit a horse. Over the years I got out of the habit of bareback riding, always using a saddle and bridle. It was when I became interested in natural horsemanship that I took it up again, riding my skewbald stallion Phillip Pembroke. It was an eye opener to realise how much I had been relying on the support of the saddle and stirrups. The walk was all right but I felt unsteady at the trot and was wary of cantering. It was as though I was a beginner again; first I would slip a little to one side, if I gripped with my legs I would bounce even more. Getting fed up steadying myself with the neck strap I thought I must stop trying so hard and do something different, so I let myself sag a little. I no longer had that desirable upright position but I could feel my backside sticking to the horse. I had made an initial connection. Gradually, and there were plenty of setbacks, I was able to stretch up without tensing. If I stretched in a rigid way I began bouncing all over again. It was only by trial and error that I discovered what to do to firstly stay on and then become comfortable. What began, as big muscle actions to keep my balance became smaller ones from more inside my body. Thinking of my breathing also helped, the more controlled and regular the less the tension.

Several days of walk and trot passed, each time my confidence growing, then I felt ready to canter. It was an anticlimax, as it turned out to be easier than the trot. The canter is a forward rolling gait, which if you survive the strike-off, almost compels you to follow. Without a saddle the three beats of the canter are easy to feel, my inside hip following the forward roll. Looking back the key to this learning process had been the realisation that if I did not change my way of sitting I was going to fall off. This jolted me out of my complacency. The resulting feel of achievement and intimacy with Phillip gave a warm glow inside that I had not felt for a long time. This is what riding was supposed to be like - fun, alive, passionate and vital. Within the confines of an outdoor school, on a schooled horse I trusted, I could still live a little dangerously! It made me realise how necessary it was to return to riding bareback to retune my balance, to relearn how to release and feel at one with my horse.

The Alexander Technique

Whilst the bareback riding reminded me to follow the horse's balance before thinking of altering it, riding with a saddle and stirrups required even more self-discipline. A saddle is a two edged sword. On the one hand it helps us to sit stiller, gives us a base of support for our feet and is more comfortable when riding for a long time. On the other hand it masks tension and allows us to become sloppy. However the horse will still feel this tension and it will be reflected in his movement. This may not be so important if our horse is fit and strong and we are not asking very much from him. If we want our horse to move to his optimum ability and comfort, especially with a performance horse, the freer we ride, the better we balance, the better he can perform. Even at the highest level there will be small corrections that the trained eye can suggest.

When I started riding the only advice I was given was 'head up, hands and heels down', which is sound advice but lacking in depth as to why and how. Thankfully there is more comprehensive instruction today based on a thorough understanding of good body use.

The Alexander Technique has helped my riding. It has helped me to soften parts of my body that I had not realised I was tightening. This instruction has been a combination of hands on work and visualisation. Everybody's own directions will differ according to individual needs, but mine might be of interest. Over the years I have become rounder in the shoulders, and wear and tear from falls has taken its toll, thus I tend to tighten in my lower back and hold tension in my shoulders and arms. I did not realise how this was affecting my horse, not so much in him going badly, but not going of his best. My directions were to think of the length from my seat bones to the top of my head, not to force myself upright but allow myself to lengthen by visualising a halo above my head. Physically this lengthening could only come from a softening of the muscles that had tightened, in my case those of the lower back and my head and neck attachment. The thought of these areas releasing was more effective than physically commanding it to happen. I had also acquired the habit many riders succumb to, that of looking down with their eyes. When I lifted my gaze and looked out into the world around, my horse went forward more readily and felt freer, especially at the canter. My final direction was to release behind my knees. I did not really know what this entailed so again I thought of that area being soft and floating. My lower leg felt as if it moved forward, that did not matter because my horse became softer and easier under the saddle. I was amazed that such little directions could have so great an effect on my horse's way of going. How the horse goes will mirror the way the rider sits. The more I became aware of how I was holding my body the more I could pinpoint the sources of tension and visualise the release.

Sometimes to give yourself body directions is not enough; a hands on approach by a qualified instructor can assist. This helped me recently at a dressage competition. I had been warming up for twenty minutes and felt I was not really deep in the saddle. I knew this because my feet were slightly reaching for the stirrups, yet the leathers were my usual length. The mere fact of going to a competition and performing in public had created tension which though minimal meant I was not riding to my best and this was reflected in my horse. Fortunately my friend who was going to call the test was an Alexander Technique teacher. I rode back to the horsebox park, where with her hands she released the tension in my hip, knee and ankle, whilst I sat on the horse. This very quiet, non-manipulative releasing is a hallmark of the technique and has to be experienced to be appreciated. As a result on re-taking my stirrups my feet felt grounded, my legs longer and more stable. Amusingly a passer by asked if I had cramp, far from it I now had the opposite. This releasing and lengthening lasted through the test, certainly helping the performance.

When the rider can join the horse's balance and become connected, and this is certainly within reach of most riders at halt and walk, it is possible to use the body to influence the horse's balance. However this often happens in a negative way when the rider hinders the horse by sitting badly.

ROSEMARY

Rosemary was having difficulty yielding her horse's hindquarters, or put another way executing a turn on the forehand. She could do one step then her horse would stop. Watching her I could see she was doing nearly everything correctly except her seat prevented more than one step at a time.

I teach this movement first at the halt and then at the walk. Rosemary began by taking up a feel on the left rein, and then asked for a slight lateral flexion with an insinuation of her left leg and left hand. Her horse responded by laterally bending at the poll and moving his ribs to the outside. He stood calmly with a slight curve along his left-hand side. As he had moved his ribs to the right he was able to stand squarely on all four legs, bent but nicely balanced, neither moving nor leaning on her hand. Her next action was to request her horse to move his left (inside) hind leg across and under his body, and then step his right hind leg to the outside. The front legs would move almost on the spot. By repeating these aids her horse would pirouette around his forehand. This is a very elementary but vitally important movement to teach your horse. Rosemary began the movement by obtaining lateral flexion, then by thinking of what she wanted followed by a slight twist in her pelvis to the left. Her horse could feel she was no longer sitting square in the saddle, this was slightly uncomfortable so if he were in harmony he would move his quarters across to square her up again. By repeating this minute twist her horse would make a succession of steps. Horse and rider would be like two dancers stepping in time; the rider's movement would become so subtle that it was invisible but still felt by the horse. Of course this degree of sensitivity is gradually attained.

On her first attempt Rosemary made a considerable twist in her pelvis also bringing back her left shoulder. Her horse did nothing so she brought her left leg into play with gentle pressure of her calf. He still took no notice so she changed hands on the rein and tapped him behind her thigh. He jumped across with this stimulation; by repeating this sequence he soon did not wait to be tapped and moved from her leg aid. Subsequently he moved from just the subtle twist in her body. This is how to teach your horse to become light and listen to imperceptible aids - by expecting him to respond to small signals but being prepared to use an effective stimulus. However Rosemary's horse would stick after one-step because she allowed his side step to slip her seat to the outside of the saddle. Thus she was no longer balanced over his balance which was over his near fore in order to move his body over. Rosemary was now sitting on top of his right hind leg making it harder for him to lift. He could still do it but there was a pause and the rhythm and flow of the movement were interrupted. To help him she needed to keep her weight to the left side of the saddle in order to counteract the centrifugal force. In this way she unburdened his right hind so he could pick it up easily. Rosemary was amazed the difference this made to the hindquarter yield when she was balanced over his balance. She was able to go from hindering him to walking him across with her seat bones - she was the leader he was the follower.

This was a simple movement performed at the halt, physically not demanding for the horse when stationary but easier for mutual understanding. In this situation it helped Rosemary to realise the importance of her seat and weight position. It also taught her about lightness, that executing this movement was not about pushing and pulling. A different weight distribution is required for all the horse's movements. Usually if the rider can accompany the horse's direction of balance the minute weight adjustments are made automatically. Once the horse and rider are balanced together it is then possible to lead the horse in the desired direction. This simple exercise, where weight distribution is so obviously important, can lead the rider to assisting the horse in all lateral movements. Once this is understood the rider will realise that longitudinal shift of balance between collection and extension also depends on how the rider sits. The horse will mirror what the rider does.

> *EVANGELIST. My sons, you have heard in the words of the truth of the gospel, that you must 'through many tribulations enter into the kingdom of heaven' And again, that 'in every city bonds and afflictions abide you;' and therefore you cannot expect that you should long go on your pilgrimage without them, in some sort or other.*
> (The Pilgrim's Progress - John Bunyan)

He did not think he was up to it, he thought he would be out of his league; he was just a riding club person. Drag hunting, just the sound of the word made him shudder; it conjured up images of charging around the countryside hopelessly out of control. The subject had come up during one of his weekly club lessons at the local riding school. He was riding Gregory, a heavy built Irish hunter and jumping rather well or so he thought. During the term progress had been steady; he and Gregory would lumber round popping the usual four fences. This week he had jumped a gate fence and a big spread. Gregory took it all in his slow careful stride - the four foot gate was his biggest jump to date. On remarking how Gregory was so slow but still easily cleared the fence, his instructor suggested, 'why don't you take him out with the university drag hounds? There are several horses going from here, then you'll see a change in him.' By the end of the lesson he had talked himself into hiring Gregory and was told to present himself at the riding school at 7.00a.m. next Wednesday, properly kitted out for a joint meet in Oxfordshire.

He did not know anybody in the university drag hunt. The class system was apparently dead and buried, the university was a meritocracy. Intellectual prowess might be the overt common denominator but undercurrents of background and upbringing were discernable in the sifting of friendships and interest groups. He had been nurtured in academic suburbia, he felt comfortable and at home in his college. The riding club was cosmopolitan in its membership, opening its arms to all; very few members even had horses back at home. On a parallel plane were those few for whom university was no interruption in their pursuit of the country sports of hunting and racing. He was not sure who they were; they had not yet touched his world, now he was to join them.

Arriving at the riding school in the dark he found his instructor just finishing Gregory's plaits. Whether it was a trick of the light or what, but Gregory seemed even bigger and more alert than usual. Soon all three hunters were loaded; he climbed in next to the driver and left the safety of the school he knew so well. He alone travelled with the horses; the other old hands were going to drive straight to the meet at a more leisurely hour. He and the driver exchanged pleasantries, after which he was left alone with his thoughts and anxieties. The borrowed black coat was hot and heavy; the stock round his neck was tight, which he dare not loosen in case he could not re-tie that tricky little knot that all hunting people knew. The further they drew away from the city the clearer the day dawned. Main roads became small roads, the flat land became gently undulating, and villages and farms replaced towns. In one of these villages they rendezvoused to pick up the other two riders and grab a quick coffee, thank goodness it was not anything stronger. The other two were friendly and welcoming, they assured him he had a good hunter in Gregory, 'only don't fall off, it'll be a long walk.' He laughed with them and felt even more queasy.

The meet was in a nearby field where thirty or forty riders were already gathered. He declined the proffered glass of port, not because he was abstemious but because he needed both hands to keep Gregory from doing anything more than circling at a walk. Underneath his fear and anxiety he was looking forward to the day, the people were friendly thanking the students for coming so far to join them. It did seem odd that for a university meet there were so few students, apparently that was normal; as not many students had the time or the money to hunt regularly, the meets were filled with local diehards. He knew this was hunting without a fox but beyond that he did not know what to expect. His new friends told him to go either at the front or the back; he naturally chose the latter believing it to be the safest and where he would not be noticed.

The line had been laid earlier by a horseman dragging a scented sack for the hounds to follow. He wished for a quiet start, so Gregory would keep relatively calm. These hopes were dashed when the huntsman blew his horn, rode off with the hounds to the far side of the field and popped over a stout looking timber fence. A few seconds later the hounds caught the scent and the air was rent with the sound of a pack in full cry. It was as startling and compelling as a peel of church bells calling the faithful to worship. Gregory answered the summons, wheeling round on the spot. An important looking man was standing up in his stirrups shouting, 'wait, wait, wait, let the hounds away please.' He had just managed to circle the prancing Gregory so he was pointing to the back, when his two companions, or more to the point Gregory's companions, flashed past along with twenty other horses all heading for the first fence.

An exasperated Gregory snatched the reins out of his hands and charged after. The first fence was completely obscured by other horses; the matter was beyond him now, it was up to Gregory. Three strides out he saw a gap open at the end of the fence line, he should be all right he thought, tightly wrapping his legs round Gregory. Two strides out a stout lady, with an even stouter expression, barged him to one side, stealing his spot. One stride out and all that was in front of him was barbed wire. Time slowed for a myriad of thoughts to flash through his mind: he must pull his horse out - he must not jump the wire - Gregory might fall or cut himself - it was not his horse - why did he think he was up to this? All his efforts to turn were met with concrete resistance by Gregory. His horse was going to jump come what may, his feeble tugs only seemed to check Gregory, causing him to put in an extra short stride right under the wire. He both felt and heard the ping as it snapped underneath his charger. Gregory went down on one knee scrabbling to stand up; he was sprawled along his neck so that he was practically eating his ears. The tingling half-fearful anticipation of a minute earlier turned to a spreading wave of dread and shame. As Gregory's large honest head lifted and popped him back in the saddle he imagined pictures of a bleeding horse, a vet stitching him by the roadside, his explanation to a grim faced instructor. He shouted to the stout lady who had checked her horse on seeing his dilemma. 'Is he cut, has he injured himself?' 'No you are lucky its old wire,' she flung back at him and galloped on. He managed to bring Gregory back to a trot, and once the others had rounded the corner he could survey the damage. There was not a mark on him; he seemed sound the only damage being a broken strap on the breastplate.

He was unsure whether to retire, but Gregory was keen and he had come a long way so he decided to carry on. By now the other riders were two fields ahead and appeared to have slowed after that first dreadful charge, he would soon catch them. He missed out the next few jumps finding a gate or a gap in each field, giving Gregory, and more to the point himself, time to recover. He cursed himself for being such an amateur, what was he doing, heaven knows where in the English countryside, riding someone else's horse which he could not control, participating in a sport in which he did not even know what you were supposed to be doing. The dread of what might have happened receded and the tingle returned as he gradually caught up the others.

Rounding a spinney, he saw the riders had stopped in the next field. As Gregory cantered down the track towards them another rider was just closing the gate into the field. Seeing the hunt again lifted Gregory's spirits and on he bounded. He knew better this time and left it to Gregory who met the gate just right and sailed over. He did pop onto his neck but with so much horse in front it was only a momentary loss of balance. Seeing the frosty look on the other rider's face he did wonder if he was supposed to have jumped it. Even if he had wanted to, he could not have stopped and besides he thought people always jumped gates out hunting. He failed to notice the beautifully built hunt jump just down from the gate. On joining the others the snatches of conversation he caught were all about the thrill of the hunt, little groups of people picking over the bones of the last twenty minutes. One came up to him, admiring his horse and remarked, 'glad to see you young chaps have still got a bit of dash.'

The hounds were quiet now as they hacked on across the fields, he wondered what would happen next, that surely was not it for the day. After a mile or so the hounds suddenly struck up again and they were off. He was still coming to terms with the new Gregory who was nothing like the steady riding school jumper. The power underneath induced both excitement and helplessness. It was difficult following Gregory's rhythm, which changed according to the ups and downs of the land and the proximity of the other horses. It was worrying him that he kept falling forward each time on landing after a jump, he had already lost his stirrup once, only just getting it back in time for the next jump. His back and legs were beginning to ache from crouching in his jumping position for so long. He could see others sitting in the saddle cantering along, he knew that was not what the books recommended but he was so tired he found himself doing the same.

Ahead he could see the riders were jumping down onto a track and up out the other side over another jump. He was not happy to jump downhill; it would be a first. Unfortunately there was a Landrover parked in front of the only gateway, he had no option but the drop. Seeing other horses disappear onto the track stimulated his horse, as if he was afraid of being left behind. Instead of slowing to a trot like the others Gregory bounded forward and gave an almighty jump. He was taken unawares and was left at the back of the saddle on take off. So bad was his timing that when Gregory landed down on the track his body was still going forward as Gregory's head and neck were coming up again. There was a clash of heads, his bowler hat coming off worst and he lost his right stirrup. Gregory was already turning slightly to the right, seeing the other horses going that way. Gregory had jumped the first fence so big that he did not have room for the comfortable stride between the two jumps and was forced to do a bounce, taking off immediately his hind feet touched down. He knew he was going to fall the moment Gregory took off because he was going straight forwards and his horse was going to the right. The force of the spring lifted his right leg over the saddle so he lay sprawled clinging onto the side of Gregory's neck, and that is how they both jumped out of the track. On landing he lost his left stirrup, Gregory's head came up pushing him upright and he landed on his feet by his horse's side who luckily had come to a stop. The man in the Landrover came rushing up spluttering, 'that was something to see lad, you were just like a stunt rider. Do you need a leg up or can you jump on as well?' He accepted the kind offer; his day was not so much fun anymore, the tingle had gone, he was tired, his head ached from the bump, how much further were they going he wondered?

Fortunately there was soon another check where he learnt they were within two miles from where they had started. He had avoided all the jumps he could since his fall, discretion being the better part of valour. His sole aim was to return to the wagon with horse and rider intact. There was no choice but to follow the others, he could see no roads and Gregory had no intention of leaving the hunt. Exhaustion, lack of confidence in his ability to stay on or even the capability of rational thought was his final undoing.

The hedge loomed ahead, it was not big; however this time there was not a convenient gate. He was resigned to the inevitable before they even took off - it became a self-fulfilling prophecy. Down he popped onto Gregory's neck, his legs swung back, he lost his stirrups and rolled onto the ground. He clung onto the reins remembering his companion's advice. He should not have bothered, then he would not have been dragged through the mud before he eventually let go. The field in which he landed had seemed small from the back of his horse, now on foot it had assumed a daunting size. He picked up his battered bowler and trudged after a rapidly disappearing Gregory. If he had known more about hunting people he might not have been so despondent; in the distance two horses turned and swam against the flow. Gregory had been caught and was being brought back. He thanked the unknown Samaritan, declined a leg up saying he would walk Gregory back the last half mile. He could see the church tower beckoning, promising sanctuary, the wagon for Gregory and tea for himself. Approaching the open field gate he realised his troubles were not yet over. Pursuing him at a rapid trot was a colossus of a bovine. His suburban mind juggled the images of himself as a toreador turning the beast, or being tossed in the air. The reality was a mad scramble through the holding mud, dragging a bewildered Gregory in a race to prevent the animal escaping. Panic struck as a dozen more compatriots raced round the corner to join in the fun. He was not going to be beaten, one last lunge and Gregory's ample bulk plugged the gateway and the enemy halted in their tracks. Safe on the road, the gate firmly closed, he surveyed the scene. The monstrous bovines now seen from the roadside were only curious Hereford bullocks. Gregory looked fine and content, though missing a brushing boot, and his breastplate hung awkwardly with it's broken strap; this day was proving expensive. He was tired, covered in mud and his bowler would never be the same again; even so he felt a glow of achievement, of dangers encountered and overcome, though may be not in the best of styles.

He attended to Gregory, rugged him up, bandaged his legs, left him picking at a hay net and proceeded to tea. A dozen stalwarts and the visitors mingled, munching sandwiches washed down with refreshing tea. They were in their host's Georgian dining room. He thought how incongruous it seemed; this collection of country folk amongst the mahogany and silver, dressed in socks, breeches and waistcoats daubed with varying amounts of mother earth - he had not been the only one to come a cropper. Strange but nice; from some distant past he remembered his best manners and joined in the conversation, recalling the day's events with the others. The stout lady was there, she did not seem nearly so fierce off her horse. She apologised for cutting him up at the first fence, and then said, 'nice to see you first timers, but you really are going to have to learn to ride cross-country if you want to do more of this. You were lucky your horse looked after you. You need to sit better, its not show jumping you know. You have got to balance him before the jump and be prepared to sit back a little, its no good throwing yourself up his neck.'

He thanked them all, made his way back to the wagon where he could collapse. On the journey home, as he drifted off to sleep, he thought - yes he had been out of his league but he would learn to sit his horse so he could have more fun next time.

* * * *

Where you go your horse goes.

Your horse most appreciates a balanced seat and good hands.

Join your balance with your horse's and lead him into your dreams.

Chapter Six

RELEASE AND REWARD

A free galloping horse is an uplifting sight. It has always stirred the heart; the thought of sitting on a horse sharing that beauty, grace and freedom has captivated people's minds throughout history. The reality has been very different. In the western world until the last fifty years, the horse has been an industrial tool; he still is in the rest of the world. His grace and beauty have been recognised and cultivated by sensitive, compassionate people since man first came across horses. Working with the horse's nature was soon recognised by all the major cavalry schools; a forced badly trained horse was an unreliable weapon. It is easy to state this but much harder to accomplish for the simple reason that horses and people are diametric opposites. The horse needs freedom, man likes to possess and control. For many people to sit on top of a horse flatters their ego, so long as they feel safe and in control. This control was achieved with a bit and bridle, the reins giving the rider something to hold and guide the horse. The bridle in the mouth seems an obvious point of control; the rider can apply pressure, cause pain and the horse will turn or stop in response. The horse however does not work like a mechanical machine; his engine is in his hind legs, which respond to messages from the brain based on feelings and instincts. Much of what the rider does arouses the instincts of survival, these tell the horse to run. He may well try that, but if the cause of his anxiety is still on his back attacking his mouth, he will fight to get rid of the rider, he will buck, rear or do whatever it takes.

The horse instinctively runs from or fights control
Man instinctively controls

By touching the very beauty he admires, man can easily destroy it. Enlightened riders have long recognised this dilemma, and try to work with not against the horse. Hence classical riding is not classical if it destroys the beauty of the horse's movement. There can not be art without grace and beauty. Just as a painting is made up of many brush strokes so that the overall effect is pleasing, so the picture of horse and rider is made up of many influences, one of which is how the rider or handler uses their hands.

Hands which Release Reward

Much has been written about hands, for many people they are central to the concept of control; in reality they should be subordinate to the mind and body, either on or off the horse. However bad hand use is a prime cause of distress to the horse. Much depends on whether the rider has an independent seat, where the hands are not disturbed by the horse's movement. Assuming the hands are under control, how well the horse understands their actions depends on the quality of feel. A good way to learn feel is dismounted without a horse.

Reins come in many forms, traditionally of natural origin such as leather or rope; though increasingly today of man made materials. A rein is like an electric conductor; some materials are better than others. Today one can buy reins of leather, plain or plaited, or with ridges, or covered in rubber all of different widths. Increasingly reins are made of artificial materials such as plastic and braided rope. Some rein materials I find have no life at all, such as plastic and rubber is not much better. Reins with ridges are for the rider who has accepted that control is still a big issue; at times in a person and horse's education this may be necessary but for general and refined riding they should not be needed. It was not until I met American and Australian horsemen that I was introduced to man made rope reins. At first I was sceptical, but I soon appreciated the life and feel of these reins. The communication was clearer both for horse and human. The weight of the reins made it clear for the horse to perceive when the rider had taken up a feel, and when it had been released. This helped me to learn how to feel for my horse. Each time my horse and I connected it was as though a bell rang, it was so distinct.

When I went back to riding with leather reins it was possible to feel more nuances of communication. The feel through the rein can be as delicate as driving a sports car, whereas often the reins are used as if driving a 4x4. This is why I like to start with a rope rein, it trains my hand. The delicacy of a leather rein is like the edge on a razor, it needs to be kept sharp and so does hand control. The feel is the same whether it's working the horse on the ground with a halter or mounted. Starting dismounted without a horse will give an idea of how the hands can communicate.

PAULINE

Pauline had an ex racehorse that could be very strong, as a consequence it was very easy for her to become embroiled in a pulling match which she inevitably lost. To try to teach her about feel and communication we each held an end of a rope rein, as long as the middle of the rein was on the ground there was no connection between us. As Pauline slid her hand down the rein the sag in the rope lifted, there came a point where she and I definitely felt connected. If she tightened the rein too much it became uncomfortable for us both; if she had not taken out enough sag the connection was too heavy and loose. This comfortable spot was where we had picked up a feel, it is like plugging in the lead on the electric kettle - connected but as yet no current switched on.

I moved my hand ever so slightly, Pauline felt it immediately. She also knew when I stopped the movement, as the comfortable feel returned. We tried the same with leather and a plastic rein. She found with the leather rein it was harder to sustain the connection, it came and went with less movement from her hand, but when she had it, it was lighter as the rein was lighter. The plastic rein was just unpleasant, it had no life. Going back to the rope rein I asked her try to follow my feel as I moved my hand. To begin with we were out of sync, sometimes pulling sometimes separated. After a while we could move around together, joined by the rein. At first both of us liked it when the connection was a little stronger. When it was too light it was wishy-washy, we both felt unconnected. After a while, as we became comfortable, this stronger feel with the tauter rein was too constricting. Then we could go back to just the weight of the rein and still feel together.

Pauline and I discussed what was going on between our hands and the rein. I asked her to consider that if she was a horse that could not talk and had no incentive to try to understand me, how could we achieve what she and I had just done? We could see the situation as one of communication and understanding, not one of coercion and confrontation. If we make a request how does the horse know it is a request and if he tries to answer it, whether he has got it right? The answer is comfort and discomfort. Of these comfort is the most important and as far as our hand is concerned that means **release**.

We played out the scenario of leading a horse on the ground with a halter and line. Pauline held one end of the rope playing the part of the horse, I held the other end picking up the feel then moved my hand for her to follow. Her reaction, as the horse, was to pull back with an equal tension - a stalemate. I kept my holding hand an equal pressure to Pauline's, as soon as she softened I gave to her. That was how she knew she had done the right thing, the pressure disappeared, the feel on the rope became comfortable once more. Pauline then asked, 'What do you do if the horse just leans on your hand and does not give to you?' I explained it was worth waiting quite a while, and then if nothing happened alter the angle of your hand and move around to the side keeping the same intensity of pressure. If still your horse leans, move round to his shoulder keeping exactly the same strength of pressure on the rope, and then make the feel intermittent with small give and takes, like prolonged vibrations. You are not tugging or jerking and must release completely when your horse gives to you. He will give his head first followed by his body. If in doubt, stop altogether, pause and begin again. Pauline practised this for a while, then we stopped and I acted the part of the horse. It might seem strange doing these things without a horse, but it is a good way to learn and there is no fear of confusing your horse if you make mistakes. The point that I want to emphasise is, that if you reward your horse when he does the right thing by releasing he is going to appreciate it. He may take advantage of your generosity and pull against you again, however if you quietly keep persevering he will eventually work out that it is nicer to follow your hand wherever it goes. Of course you are not going to do this for too long and sicken him. The best lessons are short, repeated a few times with plenty of gaps in between.

It was not long before Pauline practised leading her horse with feel. Slowly she was realising that she could lead her horse without pulling and that the release did not lose the connection with her horse's head (it was there in the weight of the lead rein) while allowing reward and a relative freedom.

This is how the hand helps the horse, connected but allowing, whatever the posture. Understanding how to use your hands is, like the rider's seat, something to **learn and practice**. We can start, like Pauline, dismounted and then when mounted begin at the halt without the interference of motion. Sit quietly with the reins resting on his neck, and then pick up one rein adjusting it to the length where you establish a comfortable connection. Your horse should be happy to stand just as he is, only moving his head when you move your hand. It is possible to ask him to turn his head towards you, away from you, lower it, lift it up all from how you move your hand. It may not feel comfortable at all to start with, that's normal, as your feel develops it will become lighter and easier. It is essential to practice on each rein separately, the feel will not be the same, and then with both reins. I must stress you

Leading the horse with a light feel and a long rein, but still connected.

are not asking your horse for flexions of the jaw or vertical bending at the poll. This exercise is for you as a rider to learn to recognise a connection between hand and nose or hand and mouth and maintain it just by the weight of the rein. The finished result feels soft and comfortable for both you and the horse. If this all new to you try it with a halter and rope reins first, then with a jointed snaffle bridle.

The horse's confirmation will always determine how he moves and thus how he must be handled and trained. How he goes will also be a reflection of the rider's personality, as these next two stories show.

DELLA

To look at her, Joy had an exemplary classical seat. She looked neat, she looked in control. That was the problem she was too much in control and this was reflected in her horse. Della was a sensitive mare with a big body and a long back. It was easy to see the driving origins in her conformation, which does not always make for a good riding horse. She was very aware of her surroundings, which meant she was often on edge. Out hacking this could lead to her never really relaxing and being impulsive. She was not dangerous but it felt as if she could explode at any minute but never did. In the school her energy looked impressive but her movement was too hurried and her attention easily wandered.

Joy found it difficult to soften her hands and give Della the freedom to allow her to stretch and relax. Joy knew she did this but could not find the way out of her dilemma. If she gave the reins Della would speed up and go on her forehand. If she kept the contact Della would over bend and try to avoid Joy's hand. Unlike Anne in the last chapter Joy did not over use her legs, she sat there like a statue. Della had a long a back and a poor hind leg conformation, because of this she did not look a connected horse. She looked as if she was made up of three separate parts - head and neck - trunk - hindquarters. Joy's hand actions did not influence Della's way of moving any further back than the withers. Her seat and leg position was not influencing Della's body and hindquarters sufficiently to develop a throughness and connection from back to front. When they did Della would move in a softer way and look whole, not a horse split into three.

Joy was stuck in a frozen inertia. She carried on doing the same thing hoping that Della would work out what she wanted, and would become light, balanced and soft in her mouth. This simply was not going to happen because she and Della were in a confrontational mindset. Furthermore Della's conformation meant she needed help to learn how to carry her rider in balance. She would speed up because her hind legs were pushing and not carrying. To help the horse find her balance I suggested Joy practice transitions and circles, using a lateral displacement of the hindquarters anytime Della hurried. This would automatically re-balance Della. In trying to balance a hurrying horse when it is in a straight line, unless done by a very skilled rider, it is easy to confuse the horse whereby the legs are saying go forward and at the same time the hands appear to be saying stop. To help Della understand, I asked Joy to walk on, adjusting the reins to a comfortable length. The first transition would be down to a halt. To counteract Joy's habit of pulling back on the rein I asked her to shorten her inside rein and lift it forward and vertically upwards. Her outside hand would remain passive but allowing the neck to bend to the inside, at the same time her inside leg and her pelvis would ask her horse to move the hindquarters to the outside. In this way the outside hind leg would be disengaged from propelling Della forward as it was now out to the side. The inside hindleg would now have moved across to underneath the belly. As a consequence it would support much more of the body weight, the three main joints of the hind leg absorb this extra weight, momentarily being compressed like a spring. The final and most important signal for Della to halt was for Joy to take her energy down by giving a sigh and relaxing completely. This was a combination of: -

1. Placing her horse in a position which transferred forward motion into a more difficult sideways movement.
2. Lifting her horse's head and neck which transferred body weight backwards.
3. A hand action which was repetitive not continuous.

These all helped Della to come to a halt without becoming confrontational i.e. a pulling match.

Joy's upward hand action was a smooth lift and release repeated until her horse stopped, this gave Della nothing concrete to fight. Joy's seat (pelvis) and inside leg aid had placed Della in a position where stop was much easier than go.

The horse has stepped underneath with his off hind, moving sideways into the halt. My aids are unilateral – right hand and leg.

This sideways halt gave Joy a basic fallback movement, by alternating sides she would exercise each inside hind leg in a bending and braking action which would go through the whole body. I did not want Joy to go round riding like this the whole time, her hand action needed to become just a soft closing and releasing which because her horse had become soft and balanced would be readily understood. However if Della was not soft and became tense and hurrying, or if Joy slipped back into her old habits this was a strategy she could use to breakdown the confrontation.

Joy's restraining hand was a reflection of tension in the rest of her body. Inside she was holding more energy than her horse found comfortable. On a lazy horse this would have helped to encourage forward movement, but on Della it was too exciting. Softening the muscles in her lower back, relaxing her jaw and slowing her breathing, brought down Joy's inner energy and that of her horse.

To an onlooker Joy had a perfect lower leg position, but it appeared lifeless. I wanted Joy to feel her legs breathe with her horse's sides and thus influence her horse's body. Her inside leg was to ask for the flexion in the ribs on a circle, her outside leg to push or guide the turn. Her leg action was not to be a continuous grip, rather at times an asking action, at times a suggesting action, at times a following action. Della needed to know Joy was talking to her whole body, not just her head and neck.

When Joy was increasingly able to ride the whole horse she found she was doing less with her hands without it being a conscious effort. She progressed from downward transitions to riding circles. Anytime Della hurried she would partly disengage the hindquarters, check the speed with a forward and upward action of the inside rein then lower her hand and release for the softness. In this way Della became accustomed to balancing herself instead of hurrying, engaging her hind legs to carry, lifting her back and stretching the muscles along her top line. Every time Della balanced herself and became light in hand I asked Joy to feel that lightness and without losing the connection with the mouth to push her hands slightly forward. As Eric Herbermann* puts it, visualise and feel you are 'pushing a tea trolley'. Thus allowing Della room to reach and stretch within a given posture while still feeling the rider's hand. In this way her hind legs would engage more but the rhythm would stay the same - she would not speed up.

The important action for both horse and rider was the release in her hand which gave Della room to stretch and soften; it stopped Joy from stiffening against her horse and fixing her hand.

---

* Eric Herbermann – distinguished international classical dressage trainer and author.

Release and Reward, at first it is a definite give of several inches but later all that's needed is a slight easing of the hands, while still keeping the feel. Joy's homework was to ride with her brain, then her body and legs and finally her hands. Only by concentrating on what she was doing would she reverse her instinct to hold and control.

WILLIAM

Christine was the opposite of Joy, she was afraid to pick up the reins for fear of hurting her horse. There is nothing nicer than riding on a long loose rein so long as your horse is balanced and listening to you. Her horse William had front legs, which were proportionately too short for the body, and he had a straight shoulder. Despite this the rest of his conformation and action produced a soft springy ride that was easy to sit. He had character and would soon decide whether he need listen to his rider. He would dawdle along with his head on the ground to the point where he would stumble and trip, as he could not lift his front legs up high or quick enough. He was a prime example of a horse on his forehand.

This horse has his weight too much on his frontlegs which may lead him to trip and stumble.

He had not started his riding career like this. When he was first backed he carried himself in a natural balance on a long rein without stumbling or leaning on the rider. Since then he had been ridden by a variety of people; he soon worked out that he need take little notice of some of these riders. He started to go on his forehand when he learnt that he could push through his rider to eat grass. In short he was a nice horse, a comfortable ride that had been allowed to slop along with his head on the ground coasting through life. He did not appear to mind when he stumbled or pulled off the odd shoe; however as a riding horse he was becoming a liability because sooner or later he would trip badly and hurt somebody. Christine was a sensitive and caring person who was aware that a bit could be painful for the horse. Most riders have to be taught not to hold on by the reins or pull on the horse's mouth. However Christine needed to take up a definite feel on William's mouth, lift up his head and neck and then give with her hands inviting him to stay in that posture.

It is not usually wise to imbue horses' minds with human qualities, but in William's case he knew exactly what he was doing. If his rider presented good qualities of leadership he would listen. He would not like it at first, then when he saw that argument achieved nothing he would settle and enjoy the higher level of stimulating interaction.

Trying not to offend Christine I explained that William had little respect for her leadership and did much as he pleased. In the school this would be a ponderous walk or a slow jog; out hacking he would either stop to eat grass or push through her to a trot if she tried to prevent this. Everybody has a different conception of what is a strong contact and what actually hurts or deadens a horse's mouth. Horses themselves will initiate pain to jerk the reins out of our hands to eat, because they know this will be brief and the reward is worth it. By meaning to be kind to William his previous riders had in fact done him a disservice, as now stronger action would be needed than if this habit had been nipped in the bud.

I rode William to show Christine what to do, beginning by riding forward at a strong walk and trot. I had to back up my discreet leg aids with an effective stimulus, by tapping him on his quarters with a short non-twangy stick. This was to sort out his impulsion problem, which was not one of innate indolence but rather a lack of respect. The taps were progressively increased in intensity, so there was no question of unjustifiably taking him by surprise. It only took two taps from me to remind him that this was how he used to respond. After that a thought, an increase in my energy and a gentle squeeze became the norm. A short sharp shock to re-establish lightness and communication is infinitely better than continual nagging, which only numbs and de-sensitises the horse. I explained to Christine that every horse was different, it was up to the rider to think through a problem to find an effective solution; with other horses that lacked impulsion even carrying a stick might be detrimental.

Riding forward with a natural posture, William's ears no lower than his withers, I picked up the reins wanting him to accept my hands connected to his mouth. Instead of jerking roughly down on me he insidiously became heavier (he respected me enough not to jerk down). This creeping gradualism is the worst because it is not blatantly confrontational, but very soon the rider is propping up the horse's head. My response was to lift both reins forwards and upwards in short staccato actions - lifting, closing my hands and releasing. These are like little pinpricks, which last a fraction of a second, irritating rather than hurting the corners of the mouth. The momentary release is what differentiates this from a vicious jerk and the upward pressure is in proportion to the weight the horse presses down. Finally, this is most important, as soon as William lifted his head my hands resumed their normal position just above his withers, nice and comfortable with a little slack in the rein. William was not going to change his habit straight away so to begin with I had to repeat this every other stride, which then stretched to every three or four. After a series of good steps he was rewarded with halts and rests on a totally loose rein. Again I must stress that such action would not have been needed if the initial training had been done correctly. Also I knew that this action was appropriate to William's temperament, it would not suit all horses. The release was the reward, the comfort for William when he walked on holding his head in a natural position, neither too high nor too low.

Christine had seen what I did and that William had eventually responded. It was going to be harder for her as she and William had developed a behavioural pattern, whereas I did not have the same history with the horse. This is why an instructor may appear miraculously to solve a difficulty; it is not always due to a superior technique. Christine still thought this was a harsh way to solve the problem, emotionally she found this difficult to accept. She could do it when I was there giving guidance, she understood the theory, she could see the result. She just could not bring herself to be so particular for long enough. Like a cat playing with a mouse William began to go on his forehand again, he knew if he put up with the discomfort Christine would give in before him; he out-patienced her. William became bilingual, if he sensed the rider had the inner resolve he would carry himself, if not he would slop along. In many cases this would not matter, but with William's conformation this way of going could end in an accident.

> CHRISTIAN. Then said Christian, Now I see that Patience has the best wisdom, and that upon many accounts: 1. Because he stays for the best things. 2. And also because he will have the glory of his when the other (Passion) has nothing but rags.
> (The Pilgrim's Progress - John Bunyan)

The trainer already had a groom, Wilhelm, but he was leaving at the end of the week then he would be on his own. Wilhelm had only stayed this long to show him the ropes, jumping was his passion and he wanted to get back to it.

'So, what are you doing here working for a dressage trainer?' he asked.

'I want to work in a top show jumping yard, the only way I can do that is if I improve my riding and have more experience working with horses, even if it's a dressage rider. Anyone who can work for this man for more than two weeks can walk into any other yard.' replied Wilhelm.

It sounded ominous and the student began to feel apprehensive.

He had first met the trainer on a course back home; it had taken all his courage to ask if he could have a summer job. Delighted and surprised when the answer had been yes, but he had heard nothing from him for five months until he rang two weeks ago asking if he could come straight away!

However good the trainer was with the horses, he was discovering he was not so particular with day to day organisation. It was not a great start when nobody was at the airport to meet him, eventually there was just he and another lady left in the arrival hall. She was the trainer's charming wife who in broken English explained the situation. It was one he soon became used to; the trainer was always late, plans always changed. He met the family, shared their evening meal and then drove to his quarters at the stables. It was a revelation to be lent a car. He protested that he had not driven on the wrong side of the road before or changed gears with a lever on the steering wheel. The reply that 'you'll learn by the time you get there', was hardly re-assuring.

He was to remember the trainer's first words to him the next day for the rest of the summer. 'You must not get upset when I shout at you, I am a nervous person, all horsemen are, I aim for perfection and keep all my energy and control for my horses.' His first job was to bring the whips out to the arena; he was allowed to stay and watch the trainer give a demonstration with his best horse. He felt elated; here was a man with magnificent horses, a brilliant rider and trainer. He was honoured to be so close to such skill and expertise; he did not know how long it would take but this was what he wanted to do.

Wilhelm was moaning because he had not been allowed to watch the demonstration, what's more the trainer accused him of losing his favourite piaffe whip. Wilhelm spent the time fruitlessly searching the large field for the whip. The trainer tore a strip off him for not finding it and threatened to make him buy a new one. An hour later the whip was found - in the back of the trainer's car. He did not apologise to Wilhelm; instead he reprimanded him for not keeping the whips in one place, counting them out and back in again. It was the groom's job to know if there was a whip in his car. The student could now see why so few grooms lasted more than two weeks.

The second day he was allowed to ride the top horse for a few minutes, under the trainer's guidance he rode a passage and piaffe. The feeling of power and energy under the saddle was frightening but so thrilling. The contained intensity had the force of a volcano but it was channelled through his hands where he held it with the lightest of touches on the thinnest of reins. He sensed he could lose it like water trickling through his fingers - gone in a trice; or it could become rough, uncomfortable, pushing at him and finally exploding. Those few moments of ecstasy gifted by the horse remained with him forever.

The next week Wilhelm left, he was now on his own, the lessons dried up. Caring for these four horses in the way the trainer demanded took all day and was exhausting. The stables were part of a large riding complex. His room was sandwiched between the trainer's horses and on the other side half a dozen stalls occupied by two-year-olds. Despite it being summer they were tied up twenty-four hours a day, each held with a ball and chain attached to the headcollar. At night he was kept awake with the noise of the chains moving up and down as the horses tried to get comfortable. After a week though, he was so tired that not even this kept him awake. Thankfully, soon after the wretched youngsters were turned out.

When the trainer sat on a horse he became a different person. He melted into the saddle and he and the horse moved as one, whether it was a relaxing walk or an energetic passage it was still the same. He disappeared into a world of his own - just him and the horse. Once, in the first few days he made the mistake of stopping to watch the master at work. He thought he had not been noticed; his punishment was to tease out the horse's tails by hand. After this he watched undetected from inside the dark stable through the window. Even so he felt guilty, not because he was neglecting his duties, but because it felt as though he were prying on private moments of intense intimacy. These were the only times, when on horseback, that the trainer seemed human.

So he was surprised one day when he rode up and said he needed his help. He felt like a stagehand being offered a leading role. Duke was a big strong chestnut who was beginning to be taught piaffe in hand. He knew it had not been going well because the trainer had been even more temperamental than usual.

'I need your help to keep him straight', was all that he said, handing him a light rein to clip on to the offside bit ring.

'I will show you what I am trying to do, then we will do it together'.

He watched the trainer leading Duke around the arena, he would walk a few yards then ask for a trot, gradually slowing the trot so Duke covered less and less ground with each stride. At the same time he would animate Duke's action with light taps on the top of his back and quarters. After a few steps of nearly trotting on the spot he would stop, praise the horse and let him stretch out at a free walk and then begin again. The problem was that Duke was so big and strong that the trainer had difficulty keeping him absolutely straight, yet still reach to tap on his back in the right spot. The student knew better than to suggest he use a longer whip, he knew from experience the favourite piaffe whip was fairly short with just the right degree of twangyness, no other would do. Every time Duke became animated with the stick he would move his head to the side, just a little, but it was enough to move the hindquarters out of alignment and the hovering steps would fade away.

The student was very nervous when he learnt what his part entailed. He was to walk with Duke, on his offside, holding the rein to straighten him if he turned in towards the trainer. Just to complicate things there was the low arena fence between him and the horse.

He could see the concentration on the trainer's face, the light in his eyes, quietly murmuring 'tac, tac, tac, ya brav', in time with Duke's feet as they lifted up and down. His next words were very different.

'Why didn't you straighten him, stupid boy'.

He thought he had, Duke's head seemed straight as far as he could tell. Duke walked round for another circuit and they tried again. The hovering steps were just beginning, one, two, three, the distance Duke advanced was now down to just six inches with each tremendous diagonal upward thrust. As the distance shortened Duke's energy grew, his veins stood out, his breathing became louder and quicker. It seemed as if he would explode, at that second the trainer relaxed, letting Duke drop down to a walk, then stopped, praised him and gave him some sugar. The student was relieved that he had not messed it up. His relief was short lived as the trainer said.

'That's how far I can get on my own, one more step and he will move his head to avoid the effort of trotting on the spot. Now you will keep him straight this time and we will get one more step - yes?'

They began again, one, two, three steps.

'Now, now, now,' hissed the trainer.

He briefly pulled on the rein each time he was asked. The first pull nothing happened, he pulled harder the next time; Duke's head turned half an inch then bent back again. At the trainer's insistence he pulled even harder, Duke turned six inches towards him and swung his quarters away. The piaffe disappeared like air in a balloon only to be replaced by the master's fury.

'Why do you pull, you are pulling, how can my horse find his balance with a fool like you pulling? You must take then give, you straighten him then give to him, you do it quick - chung, chung ya,? Do you not understand?'

He did not answer back, he knew better, he just said 'yes'.

'We will try again this afternoon, Duke is tired now, take him back', ordered the exasperated trainer.

He knew that could be anything from 1.30 - 5.00p.m. He carried on with his jobs while the small nagging pain of anxiety grew inside as the time passed. The trainer returned at 2.30p.m. took out Duke in silence and proceeded to warm him up, then he signalled for the student.

'Remember you must take enough to straighten him then give almost before he is straight so he feels nothing when he straightens. If I shout at you it is only because I want perfection, you know it means nothing', said the trainer with his charming smile. He thought to himself, 'you might say it means nothing but it does not feel like nothing when you get going'.

They began again, walking round the school gradually stimulating Duke until piaffe like steps occurred. As the steps became shorter, the trainer was at full stretch; on the horse's offside the student held the rein with a steady contact. It had taken a while to learn this contact because Duke's head would go up as he lowered his quarters. It was only when he felt a stronger tension to the side did he need to give a brief tug then instantly release. He was so anxious of making a mistake that he was nearly too late with the first correction but he made sure he released immediately.

'Good ya, good', soothed the trainer. This time Duke managed four steps nearly on the spot, then he was again rewarded with sugar.

The trainer turned to him saying, 'You did good, you are still too heavy but at least you did something, it will get better, we'll try again tonight at 6.00p.m. take him back'.

For the next two days they took Duke out for ten minutes, three times a day. The trainer explained he would learn quicker this way rather than for a longer time once a day. The student was learning to really watch the horse, now he could sense when he was about to move his head. His hand action was becoming smooth but so quick, the release was immediate. Furthermore it took so little pressure because he did something before Duke had hardly wavered. Duke was powerful, strong and chunky; he could now do six steps with ease. On one occasion he brought up so much energy he exploded, hopping forward on his hind legs like a frog. The sight of this large horse ten-foot in the air hopping alongside filled the student with awe. The trainer smiled saying, 'he can do the courbette, ya? He has such power, that is why he must learn to do piaffe correctly and not use his strength against us'.

On the fourth day he knew with certainty that he now had the right hand action. He could feel the bit through the rein, even though the contact was just the weight of the rein, he was not pulling at all; there was still a connection with the horse. He could feel when Duke swallowed and mouthed, it did not break the connection. He could also feel when the trainer's hand made a movement. He felt connected to the trainer's hand through the bit in the horse's mouth. With this depth of contact he was instantly aware when the harmony was disturbed. Whereupon he made the small, smooth, quick effective action followed by release and reward to restore the harmony. At the end of the session the trainer was all smiles.

'So now you know how to use your hand without pulling. I don't need you anymore, Duke has learned what he has to do, and I can now work him on my own and begin from the saddle. Take him back'.

The student was both thrilled and saddened. He had been terrified, useless and clumsy but he had learnt how to use his hand without pulling, jerking or being inadequate. He had learnt how to match his actions to those of the horse. He had put into practice the trainer's definition of horsemanship.

'When the horse does what I want, I do nothing. If he does not do what I want, I do something. Riding is as simple as that.'

He knew it was going to take him a long time to learn what the 'something' was, but he had made a start.

At the end of his three months abroad the high point had been those four days working with the trainer teaching Duke the piaffe in hand. His hand had done exactly what the trainer had nagged him to do. He saw this was how the trainer rode his horses, his hands were so discreet, smooth, quick and rewarding, and if you blinked you missed it. His elation might have been clouded if he knew it was to take many more years on his journey before he developed the self-discipline to nag himself.

* * * *

Ask and then allow.

Tight holding hands make tight held horses.

A small release is a large reward

Chapter Seven

TIME

Time cements the bricks of understanding

THE HORSE

Spend time together: a herd of horses, even those in stables are together twenty-four hours a day. The more time you spend with your horse the more you become part of his herd. This does not mean pestering him, it means being together but not making demands on each other. On our farm the house and buildings are situated in the middle of our land. All our horses hate going more than 300-400yds from the farmhouse, even if the grazing is better. The horses and we share the same habitat; we are part of their herd by simply living in their territory. We may not touch or handle them for days but by moving in and out of their fields, getting on with the jobs around the farm and stables we are within their bubble.

Riding through the countryside, on a long rein alone with your horse and your thoughts that is time together. Quietly holding a horse while you chat to a friend, that is being together. You can be together sharing time without pressurising each other in a variety of situations. After life itself, time is the most precious commodity on earth; sharing yours with your horse is the first step to trusting and understanding each other.

Take as much time as necessary: with horses the saying 'less haste more speed' is very apt.

Today in modern society time is money, we are all aware of how it flies by. Advances in science mean that people no longer follow nature's clock, but the horse still does. His clock is very much geared to his survival. Hence there is a time to breed (spring and summer), a time to build up food reserves (summer and autumn), a time to rest and conserve energy (winter) and a time to restart (spring). By taking him out of his natural environment and using him for our purposes there may arise conflict between our sense of time and his. Anything rushed will make him anxious, and so jeopardise the very thing we are trying to achieve. If we learn to really observe our horse he will tell us how quickly to proceed with his handling and training. This is not just in the obvious signs of discomfort such as tail swishing, flat back ears, and tense body postures; but also in the small signs of body language and behaviour. He is sending us a constant stream of information as to his physical, mental and emotional state if we can only learn to receive it. To keep our horse happy we must first follow his clock to develop trust and understanding, then we can begin to ask him to follow our clock. This means taking whatever time is necessary and being prepared to alter our time goals to adjust to our horse. I know from experience that this is really hard when we have set our heart on achieving our ambitions. The path of horsemanship is strewn with disappointments and setbacks.

Physical development is slow; horses do not finish growing and strengthening until they are at least four, and for some breeds even longer. This does not mean he cannot be handled, trained and ridden before then, but it must be done with his individual make up in mind. The more a young horse is ridden early in his life, the more years are taken off at the other end. If he is ridden before he is three his bones and joints will suffer, four is the age when he can be ridden regularly and even then he should not be asked to do too much. Real work should not begin until he is five or six. This matches well the gradual training he should have to become a schooled horse. Unfortunately this is often forgotten, especially in the competition world, hence the number of broken down and discarded horses that are barely in their teens. However big and strong he looks a young horse is still physically developing and needs to be given time.

Mental and emotional development goes hand in hand with the horse's physical state. Most behavioural problems originate from physical pain that's either been unnoticed or deliberately ignored. Box walking and weaving derive from physical confinement and isolation from the herd. Similarly wind sucking and cribbing are usually a reaction to pain in the stomach from early weaning before the foal has become used to processing only fibrous food; or being deprived of twenty-four access to fodder. Emotional anxieties are the result of physical treatment by people. In the wild, in a herd situation there are no misfits, as they would endanger the group.

As trainers and handlers if we start with a mentally and emotionally balanced horse the physical performance we are seeking will follow automatically, given the appropriate training. This means giving the horse time to trust, time to learn and time to consolidate. Handling horses from birth is generally recognised as being beneficial, but it's not always realised the young horse has a short concentration span. I don't like to handle my foals for more than ten minutes at a time, and yearlings and two year olds twenty minutes. By this I mean where I am teaching the youngster, where we are learning something specific together. Even with older horses best results come from short periods of concentration with breaks in between. This is the time to learn, you are together but it is mentally intense and if too prolonged may turn him into a robot or a rebel.

For horses with behavioural problems time is the best healer, coupled with the complete removal of the cause of the problem, usually an individual or a particular environment. Nowadays we tend to try to solve problems head on, thinking to save time whereas my past teachers would advise turning a horse away for six months to let it down, give it time to learn to be a horse again, cleanse away the worries and anxieties. After this, start right from the beginning and put the foundations right.

THE PERSON

This can be divided into how long it takes to learn to sit on a horse and control him, and the time it takes to learn how to teach and train him for whatever purpose we have in mind. It is a dual subject of riding and training and requires a mental and physical ability, because there is no doubt that a good rider improves a horse's education just by sitting on him; conversely a poor rider can soon ruin a horse. Fortunately the horse is a very forgiving creature, and if a person goes at their own pace and that of the horse, the majority of us can learn sufficient skills to make riding enjoyable for both parties.

Physical Time

There is no doubt that the younger you start the easier it is to learn to ride. Young bodies are not set and are naturally looser and more capable of following the horse's motion. If children fall off, which will happen as part of learning, they bounce easier and are not so fearful of remounting. Having said that, with the right instruction and a reliable horse, adults can acquire the necessary skills to learn an independent seat. It all depends if the adult can ride often enough, two or three hours a week is not sufficient. If this is all you can manage because of your lifestyle don't despair, you can still progress if you can arrange a holiday week, where you will be in the saddle and handling horses all day long. In this way you can leap frog up to a higher plateau of ability, then consolidate that skill in the following weeks before you can have another intense session. So think of this as a cycle of improving and maintaining. It is possible to become competent enough to make riding enjoyable in a relatively short time, but to develop subtlety and finesse is a permanent on going process.

Mental Time
Progress in both riding and training your horse will depend on mental ability to learn. Apart from a few naturals, for the majority of us skill comes from understanding what we are trying to achieve, being told or telling ourselves what to do and then practicing. After you have acquired a certain level of technical skill riding is a mind game; the naturals do it instinctively, the rest of us have to learn. How long this will take depends on the quality of instruction, your individual dedication, and the ability to recognise when you have got stuck and need to try something different. It is quite possible to carry on for years being reasonably competent but not quite hitting the mark either as a rider or trainer. But if, as it was for me, this leaves you dissatisfied you will want to search for the answers. Nearly always the answer lies inside us. Constant self-scrutiny and mental flexibility are needed. For some this may mean going from trainer to trainer, trying system after system, others may hit on just one thing that triggers the 'light bulb' moment. Becoming closer to your horse, understanding him, helping him is an ongoing thing and therein lies the fascination.

These next couple of studies illustrate how the horse dictated the pace of progress, how the handler recognised their own level of skill and opportunity and adjusted accordingly. Trailer or box loading is one of the most common and frustrating problems that people encounter.

CASPIAN

Caspian was a useful working hunter type of pony, just right for a young teenager to develop confidence and start competing. The only trouble was he did not like going in the trailer, and if he did he would shoot out backwards before anyone could put up the back bar. Once he was in, although anxious he did not try to break out until it was time to unload, then he would shoot down the front ramp knocking over the handler, ripping rugs; he did not care if he injured himself he just had to get out. Even though he was Charlotte's pony, as in many family's it was mum and dad who did much of the handling. Certainly to begin with, it was mum Barbara who would be doing the loading. Watching the family working with Caspian I could see that he was an anxious pony who wanted to please, but if his anxiety level became too high he would just start to run. When ridden he would respect the bridle enough not to physically run away, but his mind would be still running. This was shown in the tension he carried - hurried stride, tightness in his top line and an artificially held position of head and neck. He was not like this all the time and Charlotte had made a great improvement in the short time she had owned him but his underlying anxiety would easily surface.

Rather than take him straight to the trailer I wanted to do some groundwork to try to understand him and build up a trust and a language, which I could use in order to load him into the trailer. Caspian was naturally on the defensive and as with other horses this can be expressed either by wanting to move away or by pushing on the handler. My first job was to be able to keep him from pushing on me; he would do this very subtly. In leading him around the arena he would quietly try to dictate where we walked by gently nudging me with his shoulder. It was so easy to step out of his way, conceding a few inches so that by the time we had walked 30yds he had moved me 8ft off the track. This was his anxiety being expressed in an offensive manner, an insidious 'strike first before they get you' syndrome. It also confirmed his belief that he was the leader as he was controlling my direction, and this would soon degenerate to my speed as well. As with the other horses you have read about, my groundwork consists of first developing trust, sometimes this means doing nothing just gentling, calming and re-assuring. At other times it means gaining his respect so I am viewed as his leader by proving to him I can move him around, how it is done will vary from horse to horse. As Caspian was anxious by nature I wanted to keep it as low key as possible and only raise the level of energy gradually. Slowly he learnt to bend and circle at the walk, change direction, stop and back up. These are the basic yields, which help him to soften and give to me both in body and mind. As he liked to threaten me with his shoulder I had to first defend myself by bumping it with the back of my hand; immediately he jumped away showing his anxious side again, which I ignored and carried on walking. To re-enforce that I was the one in charge I circled him at the walk, giving him about 6ft of rope and walking a small circle myself, so he did not have to turn too tightly. If I turned and walked towards his shoulder, directing my energy at it, even touching him lightly with the tail end of the rope, he should pick up my body language and move sideways away from me for a step or two. That was all I wanted, him to allow me to drive his forehand away. Once Caspian would move easily for me at the walk it was time to ask the same at the trot. With this higher level of energy he was much more inclined to try to run away, it took several sequences of walk to trot and trot to walk transitions before he was settled.

After 30 mins. I felt Caspian and I understood each other enough to try the trailer loading.

Approaching the trailer was enough to put Caspian on his guard, his head went up, and he did not even want to look at it. There are many ways of loading a horse; I have seen most of them at some time or another. They include tempting the horse with buckets of feed, hitting him hard on the quarters, passing lunge ropes behind him and pulling him in, waiting and doing nothing, making life outside the trailer so uncomfortable he would rather be in the trailer; the variations are numerous. The key factors are trust and time.

First of all I took all the partitions out, removed the breast bar and opened the front ramp. A trailer or horsebox is a claustrophobic place for a horse. For a prey animal any enclosed space puts him in a vulnerable position so it must be treated with extreme caution. If previous experiences have been frightening, either because of the methods used to get him in or the resultant journey, he will understandably not want to go in again. What is needed is time and understanding by the handler, any impatience, exasperation or loss of temper will only confirm the horse's suspicions. Of course this is often how we feel if he won't load, then the more we push the horse the worse he behaves, we feel the pressure of time. We can train our horse to trailer load so that it is a comfortable experience. With a horse like Caspian it was doubly important that I should feel no pressure of time and expect only a little. I led him up to the ramp and waited for him to acknowledge its existence; unless he lowered his head to look at it and perhaps sniff it he was not even in a start position.

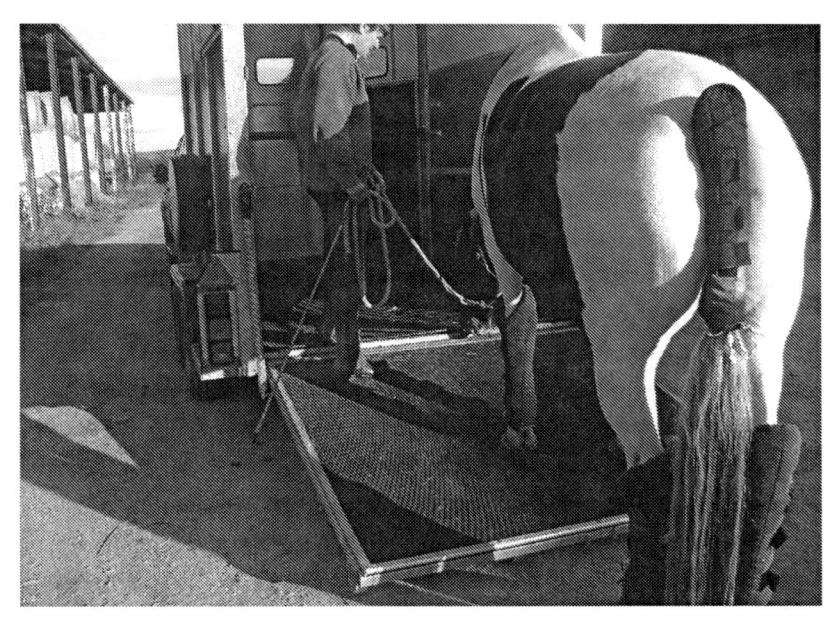

The horse is inspecting the ramp and is now mentally prepared to think about what the handler wants who is calm, confident and relaxed.

He backed off several times, I repositioned him by lightly tapping him on top of his quarters, as soon as he took a step forward this was rewarded by stroking him with the stick on exactly the same spot where I had tapped him. I wanted him to view the stick like my hand - it could stimulate or stroke and soothe. I must stress that I had done considerable work away from the trailer gentling Caspian with the stick so he would see it as a long arm and show no fear. I had also taught him that like my arm it could stimulate with increasing rhythmic movements culminating in small taps and it could rub him to reward a try. By rewarding his slightest step forward and allowing him to stop, he was given time to feel more comfortable with the trailer. After several backwards and forwards he walked into the completely empty trailer where there was a small reward of carrots, which he quietly ate. This in itself is a sign of a degree of relaxation; an anxious horse will not eat, which is why bribery often fails. Such an in and out approach might be easier for people to understand if they put themselves in the horse's place and imagine the trailer is a cupboard. Left to your own devices you might look inside then bring your head out to look around outside. Next you might step inside with one foot then step out again; finally you might step completely in, even nearly closing the door but not quite, so you have an escape route. As you become comfortable in the small dark space you might close the door completely. On the other hand if someone started shouting at you to get in the cupboard and pushed and shoved, you would fight back. If they did put you in and then locked the door you would be even more desperate. Certainly the next time you would be even more reluctant. This was how it had been for Caspian.

He stayed inside for a while then I asked him to walk down the front ramp. At this he rushed past and dragged me down the yard - leaving by the front door certainly upset him. Barbara had got this far loading him; it was when the partitions were in that she could not prevent him shooting back out again. I had wanted to start right from the beginning so I could observe his behaviour and show Barbara the principles of rewarding a try however small. With the breast bar and the partition in place Caspian was even more reluctant. He went part way in and out at least twenty times before he felt comfortable enough to go right in. My actions had to walk the fine line between cajoling and coercing. I had remained at the top of the ramp and he had walked past me to go in the trailer, so in this position I could put the back bar up behind him. The mere fact of me standing there, even though I was stroking his quarters and soothing him, was enough for him to shoot out once more. In this situation it was important not try to hold him in by force and put up the bar, that would only worsen his claustrophobia.

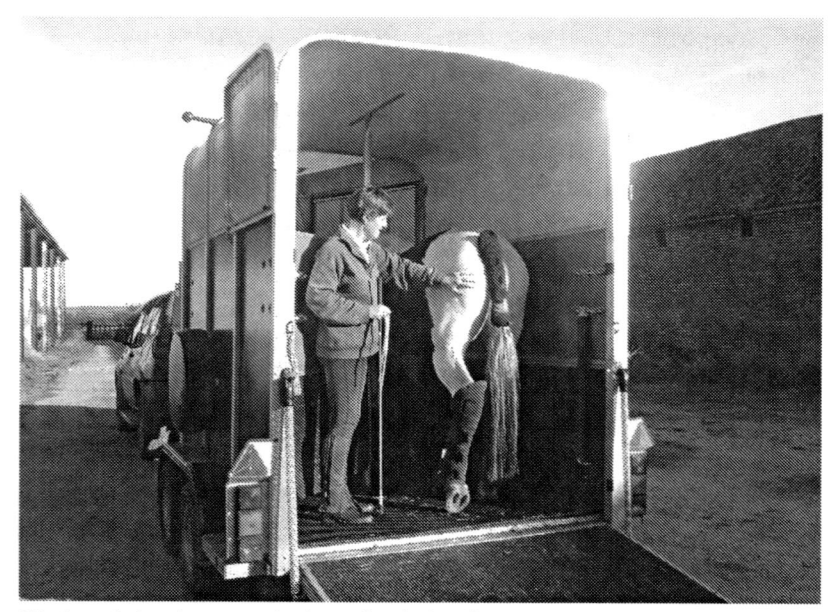

The horse is learning to stay in the trailer, the handler quietly rubs the quarters but does not try to keep the horse in or quickly lift the back bar.

When he would stay in for ten seconds I invited him to back out and left him standing while I talked to Barbara, thus removing all pressure and the weight of expectation. Little by little he would allow me to lift up the bar and touch him with it and put it down again. Soon after that I could drop the bar in its slot, he knew it was there and accepted it There were little set backs, not to worry, I just started again and built up to where we had got. In fact once he was shut in he appeared quite resigned and quietly ate his hay. His problem was in the actual loading and unloading, no doubt due to past bad experiences. So for now we left trying to unload him out the front; since he was calm backing out, I thought it better to build up his confidence in all aspects of his training and come back to that in the future, when it may well have disappeared by itself.

In all it had taken about an hour for me to load Caspian and close up the ramp, now it was Barbara's turn. Barbara found it hard to get Caspian to the start position at the bottom of the ramp, he would swing his quarters away and try and back off. She quietly re-presented him, stroked him when he stood in place, it was a battle of wills. If she lost her temper and was to hit him rather than encourage him, he would be justified in his anxiety and would follow his instincts of survival. On the other hand, if she was too indeterminate and did not present clear calm implacable leadership, Caspian would know if he danced around long enough she would give up or lose her temper. Caspian was a mix of both anxiety and non co-operation. It was up to Barbara to closely observe his body language and behaviour and act accordingly, to keep him just below his boiling point and reward any small progress. With me giving guidance she managed to load him and put up the back bar whereupon we finished for the day on this good note.

When I came back a couple of weeks later the situation had deteriorated. Caspian would swing his quarters around the side of the ramp and then lunge on the rope and pull Barbara down the yard. He did not respect her ground handling skills and soon found a weakness and pushed through it. He also sensed that she did not quite believe that she could do this without my guidance. Horses quickly pick up our inner feelings and thoughts, especially negative ones. Handling horses is a combination of technical skill and mental agility.

To improve Barbara's technical skill I asked her to go back to the arena and work Caspian in the basic yields. She needed to prove to him that she could control where and how he moved. Certain yields have a stronger effect in developing mutual respect; the better he would back up, move sideways and yield away from her with both his forehand and hindquarters the more likely he was to follow her wishes in other movements. To a certain extent Barbara was still learning to see the small signs that he was either going to push on her or take-off. If these are spotted soon enough it is much easier to nip them in the bud with little effort before things get out of hand. In other words Barbara needed to do more homework away from the trailer to build up trust, understanding and respect. We also made it easier by parking the trailer along side a wall so Caspian could only swing one way, although eventually she would have to load him in the open. On returning to the trailer Barbara succeeded in loading him but could not put up the back bar; he did not yet feel comfortable and soon discovered a chink in her armour - that little moment when she took her concentration from him in order to lift up the bar. The important thing was for her not to worry, just start all over again, telling herself she had as long as it would take. Often when the handler mentally resign themselves to being there for the rest of the day, completely clearing their mind of the other things they could be doing, the hole in their mental armour is mended. The horse senses this and accepts their leadership, if you are mentally totally convinced you will accomplish the task, it will happen much sooner than you thought. Barbara found the feeling of eventual certainty and Caspian accepted the inevitable, allowing her to put up the bar on the fifth attempt. At this she stroked him and removed the bar while his mind as well as his body was still in the trailer, then she invited him to back out and finished for the day.

Barbara took it slowly over the next month; she wanted to consolidate for both of them the act of going in the trailer, then becoming comfortable even nonchalant with the process. Each time there was a reward in the trailer, which was never used to coax Caspian, but to confirm that being inside was a nice place to go. The final step was to drive him somewhere, unload him and then reload him and come home. She only drove 30yards the first time gradually building up to such a distance that it would have been difficult to walk Caspian home. Thus Barbara was committed to loading him, adding more pressure, but the time had consolidated the training and all went well.

Taking time had been essential for both Barbara and Caspian. Time for the pony to get over his fear, both of the trailer and the pressure people might put on him. Time for Barbara to understand and observe Caspian's behaviour, time for her to acquire the technical competence to handle him, time for her to develop the necessary mental strength and confidence. Caspian had been frightened in the past, that fear had left a permanent mark in his mind; it was only his trust and acceptance of Barbara, which would override that fear. The longer the good experiences lasted the more the fear would recede but it would never be totally cleansed.

ROCKY

This study is also about trailer loading, where taking time was no problem so it did not take much time at all.

Rocky was an orphaned foal, rescued at six weeks. Jo had reared him, neither spoiling nor neglecting him. He was well integrated with the other horses in the paddock, they had taught him equine manners. Jo had backed him over one summer when he was three, she was constantly surprised how understanding and co-operative he was compared to other older horses she had taken on. This was not so surprising since Rocky had known Jo since birth and she had never caused him any fear - he was a blank sheet for her to write on. The only slight problem was that Rocky had grown from a cute appealing foal into a large friendly heavyweight cob. Not a problem in itself except that Jo had a single horse trailer that would fit Rocky like a glove. I did not need to help Jo she knew what to do.

She left the trailer in the field for Rocky to inspect, the ramps were down, he would walk in and out just from curiosity. Consequently it was no problem to lead him through or to ask him to stand and quietly eat a small feed inside. Step by step Jo began to close up the trailer starting with the breast and back bars. Rocky would happily keep munching on his hay. He only began to show anxiety if she started to close the top door at the front. Jo was in no hurry so she would half close the door talking to Rocky, and then open it after a few seconds. Within a week this progressed to holding it shut for a short time. Rocky soon lost the anxiety, he always had a pleasurable time in the trailer, he had something to eat and it did not last for long. The next step was to hitch up the trailer, turn on the car engine and let Rocky feel the trailer move. Step by step, with plenty of time to assimilate each new experience, Jo trained Rocky to load and be transported in only a few weeks. Since she was in no hurry, entering the trailer was always a pleasurable experience; it was something Rocky looked forward to. Rocky had a natural trust and curiosity so he saw trailer trips as something of interest; he saw a wider world, met other horses and always came home again. It soon became a regular sight to see this narrow trailer with a large horse's bum bulging out the back. Jo went about the training in an unhurried sensible way, letting Rocky dictate the pace. He became quite happy to be wrapped in a girdle of metal and driven away. Eventually Jo bought a bigger trailer to take two at a time; we all missed seeing Rocky drive by.

> INTERPRETER. *Therefore Passion had not so much reason to laugh at Patience because he had his good things first, as Patience will have to laugh at Passion because he had his best things last.*
> (The Pilgrim's Progress. John Bunyan)

It had seemed strange but re-assuringly familiar when he returned to Arthur's in November. He had not been to the farm since March. Since then the hectic turbulence of his life had pushed last winter's riding out to a distant memory.

Arthur had not changed he looked exactly the same. He wore the same coat, which unsuccessfully struggled to meet in the front. The same battered cap covered the silvery strands of hair. He walked with the rolling gait of a farmer who had seen too many winters. But the twinkle was still in his eye; he spoke with a deep rich voice giving him an ageless and timeless quality, to be found only in the best of wines.

He was in his parallel universe once more, a welcome antidote to the frenzy of college life. Reg was tacking up the horses, he could see that he was 'carrying a bit of overweight'. Reg had summered well and was counting on exercising the pointers to lose it. Characteristically he was already moaning that Arthur should have got the horses up sooner, and how were they going to get them fit for hunting let alone racing at the beginning of February.

Arthur muttered, 'well we had to wait for our student jockey, didn't we?'

He knew them well enough to realise that it was the pressure of autumn farm work that had caused the delay, nothing to do with him.

It was a new season and it rekindled his hopes. He had first heard of Arthur a year ago from a fellow student who was already a point-to-point rider.

'There's this farmer a few miles out who's looking for some help exercising, you never know he might lend you a horse for the university race.'

He knew there was not a chance last season. Arthur hardly knew him; he had never ridden racehorses before let alone jumped a chasing fence. All the same the spark of hope, not completely extinguished, was quietly fanned in his fantasies. Maybe this year he would get a chance. Part of him hoped not, as he knew he was not ready. Another part, wherein lay his sense of excitement, adventure and passion, desperately wanted a go. This was his eternal dual between sense and sensibility. Should he mention it to Arthur? He decided not as it would be an embarrassment for Arthur to have to say no. Anyway Arthur knew about the university race, if he thought it was right for him to ride one of his horses he would say so and enter them.

After a summer of working with strong muscular dressage horses it was a satisfying change returning to the lighter, angular thoroughbreds, to hitch up his irons and get his bum out the saddle. Riding out that first morning Reg filled him in with all the local gossip, in the countryside such benign curiosity oiled the wheels of life. Although to his innocent ears he found it hard to believe some of Reg's stories of love and lust. In return he was expected to reveal the juicy bits of student life. He was sure they did not believe him when he insisted that his was a tame existence compared to theirs. Then the grass always seems greener on the other side. More to the point Arthur had brought up a new young horse. They had great hopes for this gelding, he being related to the really good horse Arthur ran five or six years ago. Racing people are eternal optimists believing each new horse will be 'the one'. His course this year was less demanding so he would be able to ride out at least three times a week. He soon slotted into the old routine, though his muscles ached for the first week.

One Saturday he was invited to stay for lunch where he met more of the family; Arthur's son was back for the day from agricultural college. During the meal Arthur let slip they were going to castrate some calves that afternoon, 'could you give 'em a hand, it'd be easier with the three of you?' Well he could hardly so no after such a lovely meal, and Arthur did say they were just calves, it should not take very long. His knowledge of farm livestock was extremely limited, so what had looked like cute scampering calves when he rode past the shed became very different on closer inspection. These beasts were more than a few weeks old; they were big, well muscled and bright eyed. In fact as soon as he, Reg and Arthur's son Mike approached the gate the dozen calves turned tail racing around the shed bucking and kicking with great glee. Arthur always saved up these jobs for when his son was home and anybody else who could be persuaded to help.

Reg and Mike showed him how to catch one of the calves. Reg herded him along the back wall towards Mike, as he shot past Mike grabbed him round the neck, knocked him off balance at the shoulder and deftly grabbed a front leg. The calf plopped down into the deep bed of straw where Reg pinned down his back legs, he stopped struggling lying inert awaiting his fate.

'Quick grab the nippers, there on the gate,' urged Mike.

He had been wondering how this unkindest of cuts would be done, despite Reg's stories of knives and teeth, he knew it would be more humane in the C20th. Hanging on the gate was what looked like a pair of garden shears but instead of cutting blades were two wide smooth edges like brake blocks. These smooth edges would painlessly crush the cords of fecundity. They were properly called a Burdizzo, no doubt invented by some fiendish East European scientist. The job was quickly done with little resistance from the calf, barely leaving a mark. He sprang up, stood bewildered as if more than his feelings had been hurt but not knowing quite how.

'Now it's your turn,' said Reg, 'we'll send him to you and then you grab him.'

He had never been very good at catching a cricket ball at school, but this time at least he would see it coming. The calf rushed past, he stretched out a hand missing the neck and ended up clutching the poor animal around the middle, who jack-knifed in the air, kicked him and sent him sprawling in the straw. With great glee the lads drove another his way, this time he hung onto the neck and was dragged round the shed before he had to let go - two nil to the calves. While he got his breath back the others caught a couple more. By now their taunts were beginning to sting, he would just have to dive in, flip the calf, job done. He remembered learning to tackle at rugby - you dived in low and hard with no thought to your own safety. He nailed the next one in great style, accompanied by a loud cheer from Reg and Mike. As they worked their way through the dozen, the remaining ones became more elusive. The last of these had watched his compatriots being felled and was having none of it; he was the biggest and twisted and turned like an eel. All three of them hit the deck before he was finally caught. Afterwards they sat recovering in the straw, he was down to his shirts sleeves, panting and covered in sweat, aching all over from the kicks and bruises. He would not have missed it for anything, he felt like he did on the top of a mountain - alive.

'Well you're not bad for a townie,' praised Mike.

Later having tea round the kitchen table, not only had the food never tasted better but now he felt accepted as more than just a student rider.

His jumping had improved since his initial efforts out drag hunting. In the summer term he had practiced over cross-country jumps and even ridden in a couple of hunter trials. However he had yet to jump at speed. Before the first race of the season Arthur took two of his horses for schooling over proper sized fences with their race day jockey. This was essential for the young horse so he would get an idea of what to expect in a race. This was a crucial time in his education where it was vital he was not pushed too quickly or he would lose confidence. Both horses were entered in next week's races; they were lean, alert but not yet hard fit. They needed a couple of races under their belts then they would peak in about a month's time. Their feed was home grown oats and beans with raw eggs and a bottle of Guinness. Arthur was a good old-fashioned feeder epitomizing the saying 'the eye of the master feeds the horse'. The horses reflected his skill in their shining coats and bright eyes.

He had never been to a point-to-point and not where he was involved with any of the horses. The horses knew it was a race day; they were even more on their toes than usual. They were unrecognisable, plaited and wearing their bright new travelling rugs. Reg was wearing his best tweed jacket and cap. Arthur supervised the loading and left them to take the box to the racecourse. Reg had told him that a point-to-point was like a picnic whereas a proper National Hunt meeting was like a sit down meal. That did not mean it was any less serious but more informal and friendly.

The excitement started with seeing the horses in the paddock, sleek, fit and on their toes. His horse (that was how he thought of him), who had back at the farm seemed an impressive combination of power, energy and beauty, was now just one of a dozen similar magnificent creatures. Some prowled round like panthers, others jogged round heads in the air, eyes rolling, some were cool as cucumbers others were already sweated up their necks covered in a white lather. He found it hard to believe that he had actually ridden one of these. It was equally incredulous that anyone would get on their backs and gallop for three miles over big birch fences. But sure enough out came the jockeys each to join the small huddle of people connected with their mount. There was Arthur and a couple of his racing friends. Arthur was unrecognisable in his best country suit and hat, quietly checking the girths and giving the jockey last minute instructions while Reg held the impatient horse.

There was a lull as the horses cantered down to look at the first fence; the crowd left the paddock to get a better viewpoint or put on last minute bets. He made his way to the first fence. The tension raised another notch as the horses lined up at the start, or rather failed to. The starter a portly red-faced man with a bowler hat was becoming increasingly exasperated. Several times he had asked the jockeys to bring their horses into line only to have one errant horse wheel round and the jockey cry out, 'please sir I'm not ready'. Finally he got as good a line as he was going to get and dropped his flag.

Initially, he just saw the horses as a distant bunch coming towards his fence, and then he could hear the thundering of their hooves. Within seconds they were only

50 yards away and he could feel them through the ground as well as hear them. No wonder infantrymen used to quake at a cavalry charge. The noise reached a crescendo over the jump, jockeys urging on reluctant mounts, the breaking of the birch as the horses brushed through the top of the fence and the crash as a couple of horses fell. In a few seconds it was all quiet as the cavalcade raced onto the next fence; the fallen horse had scrambled to its feet and cantered after as the jockey watched in frustration. The cries of the crowd died down to be replaced by the sound of the commentator. Arthur's horse it appeared was lying near the back of the field. In what seemed no time at all they came round for a second time but now there were only eight left in the race, some had fallen others had been pulled up after one circuit. As the horses were now spread out he watched each horse jump; the first three cleared the fence effortlessly without checking their stride. Of the rest, one got too close, one stood back so far he crashed through the top of the birch, pecked badly on landing and pitched his jockey over his head. Arthur's horse jinked coming into the fence so was forced to jump at an angle, thus lost ground and dropped back to second last.

He followed the stream of people rushing to get a view of the finish. Coming to the last there were only three horses making a race of it. Arthur's was back in fifth and appeared to have run out of steam. He knew Arthur had entered his horse just to give him a run to gain experience, all the same he was disappointed; the excitement of the occasion had been infectious. He and Reg went to meet their horse as he crossed the finish; Arthur came puffing up a little behind them. The jockey as if to ward off criticism said, 'he didn't get the trip, gov.'

'I know, I didn't expect him to yet,' grumbled Arthur, 'couldn't you hold him straight at them jumps?'

'It's only his first race, he's still learning the game,' replied the jockey, 'he needs more schooling alongside a good horse.' Arthur's other horse ran in a later race, he too needing a run came in near the back of the field

By the time they had driven home, made the horses comfortable and gone in for tea Arthur had cheered up. The whole family picked over the bones of the day, drawing what comfort they could and being philosophical over the disappointments, thus rekindling hope for the next time. Arthur's choices for the next meeting were now much clearer.

'The old horse is down for the Open, he's too good for the student race, and the young'un needs more schooling.'

Relief was his main emotion with a slight taint of disappointment. After seeing the races today he knew for him to ride would be like taking a moped in the Manx TT. He put all thoughts of racing to one side for the time being.

* * * *

The riding club president, a past Olympian, had advised him, 'don't specialise too soon, get as broad an experience with horses as possible.' This he had done for a couple of years, during which his debate continued between the passion, which loved the thrill of speed, the crescendo of jumping; and the cerebral which sought perfection and harmony in the schooling and training. He soon bought his own horse - Pharaoh, a 16.1hh Thoroughbred 3 year old. He backed him, brought him on and then took him hunting. Over the stonewalls of the north they both learnt to jump. He and Pharaoh suited each other; the horse was bold with a big jump and instant acceleration. He preferred to be calming and soothing a horse rather than pushing or driving. One spring day saw them at a hunter trial, which included a point-to-point fence. It was the biggest fence he had ever contemplated jumping and it pressed the tingle button in his stomach. In his excitement and fear he kicked hard three strides out. Pharaoh responded instantly, covering the distance in two long ones and took off. The power under the saddle was phenomenal, like an ejector seat, fortunately he had learnt to sit back and push his legs forward on landing.

Out of this grew the kernel of an aspiration, gestating throughout the summer to become a possibility in the winter. He would do what Pharaoh was bred for, take him pointing. He talked to friends already in the game, schooled Pharaoh over jumps, got both of them fighting fit. The preparation was thorough, they had a trial outing where he pulled up after a circuit, and the next time would be for real.

Two weeks later sitting in the changing room a jumble of thoughts flashed through his mind - what if he fell, what if they both fell, had he the strength for two circuits, maybe he could win, how could the other jockeys look so calm laughing and joking? When the call came for jockeys he felt drained with apprehension. At last after the interminable wait he was in the saddle and cantering down to look at the first fence. Pharaoh knew what was coming and was stronger than ever.

Circling at the start he hung to the back, so much so that the starter asked if he was ready. This was a deliberate choice as two weeks ago he had not been able to hold Pharaoh and jumped into the lead over the first fence. This time he wanted to avoid the melee and give him time to settle. The flag went down, the others jumped off almost in line, he held Pharaoh a moment longer then released him as the starter's assistant cracked his hunting whip to give him added impetus. Even so going into the first he had nearly caught up with the next horse. For the whole of the first circuit he kept to the back and to the outside. This way Pharaoh would get a clear view of each fence and there would be little risk of being brought down by fallen or refusing horses. Of course they would also gallop several hundred yards more than if they kept to the inside but for a first race discretion was the better part of valour.

Each fence was a mini-Everest to be planned for, climbed and descended. Just like mountaineering racing has many uncontrollable dangers. Two weeks ago the practice circuit had been a nightmare. All he could do was try to stay on and point Pharaoh at the fences, he was not sufficiently in control of either himself or the horse to have any say in the take-off spot. Consequently they really stood back at some fences and got too close to others. Luckily Pharaoh saved the day for him by jumping straight and learning quickly so by the time he pulled up the horse had learnt to jump at speed. That had been the problem; Pharaoh had little experience of how fast the horses galloped in a race or the excitement this would raise and it had been the same for his jockey. He had watched races but it was nothing like actually doing it, which had been a shock and a thrill for him.

As the fences ticked by he and Pharaoh began to get a rhythm, he was starting to see the stride. He could tell if Pharaoh was going to stand off and put in one of his gigantic leaps taking off fifteen foot before the fence. Thankfully he only did that a few times after which he became better at arriving at the right spot of his own accord. Going into each fence he would crouch a little closer to the saddle and squeeze with his legs, more for his own stability and confidence than to help Pharaoh. This certainly helped on landing when Pharaoh's head would disappear as he reached down and forward to regain balance and resume galloping.

Beginning the second circuit there were four horses in a bunch at the front with the rest becoming strung out behind. Without him pushing at all Pharaoh was slowly catching up the leaders, gaining a couple of lengths with each jump. Three fences from home the leader kicked on, followed by the other three trying to keep in touch. By now Pharaoh had moved into contention alongside the fourth; coming to the last he was in second place, the leader appeared to have slowed or he wondered was Pharaoh just going faster. Landing in the lead over the last his first thought was, thank goodness they had both survived all the fences. The finish was two hundred yards up a slight rise, a real test of stamina for the tiring horses. He knew he would have to ride for the line; he could hear and sense the other horse just behind.

Pharaoh was tiring and so was he; with each stride he tried to crouch and push and squeeze with his legs while stretching forward his arms, scrubbing the horse along. He knew not to throw the reins away, with every stride he tried to gather Pharaoh up and throw him forward. His legs were burning with the strength sapping effort, he could feel the once iron muscles were slowly turning to jelly. He was gasping for every breath, his lungs on fire; a sensation he had not experienced since sprinting for the finish at the end of a five-mile cross-country race. It had been hell then and was now, but he only had to hang on for a few more seconds.

The crowd funnelled them towards the line; the other horse was now alongside. Cocooned in the noise of the panting horses the cries of the crowd were just an orchestral background. He tried to push harder, he could not; Pharaoh was now carrying him along rather than he riding him out - he was a mere passenger. He knew he had lost as they crossed the line, the official distance a neck. Walking to the second bay in the winner's enclosure, a curate's egg of a place, a disconsolate punter shouted to him, 'you should object you were run out.' A smile grew inside, yes he was disappointed not to have won, but even more he was elated at the thrill of the whole experience from getting Pharaoh fit to culminating in the excitement and fear of the race itself. He would never be the sort of jockey who could get on any horse at a moment's notice; this had been him and Pharaoh together.

It had taken ten years since he first dreamt of riding in a race at Arthur's yard. He had needed that time to learn about life, to learn about farming, and to continue his journey of horsemanship. It was a late harvest but one of the best.

* * * *

The more time you spend with your horse the better - become part of his herd.

Your horse will tell you how long he needs - so be adjustable.

The less demanding you are at the start of his life the more years you add on the other end.

Time is the best healer - physically, mentally and emotionally.

The time it takes to learn basic handling and riding skills varies with each person. It is a continual process - enjoy it.

Chapter Eight

CONNECTING - FEEL

This is the chapter where I shall try to draw together the threads of horsemanship discussed so far. We often hear phrases such as:-

'He really has a way with horses, they'll do anything for him'.
Or
   'She has a real feel for a horse'.

What have these people got that others have not? Some people are just naturals and probably could not put into words what they do. The rest with hours of observation, dedication and practice have connected with their horse in mind and body for a common purpose.

The Mental Connection
Rather than viewing the horse as a machine, the aspiring horseman tunes into what his horse is telling him and realises that his horse is doing exactly the same. The first stage is observing and interpreting the horse's body language and behaviour - in order to understand him. Is he interested or frightened, is he pushy or curious and friendly? It is important while doing this not to endow the horse with human qualities; he is only able to just be a horse. The way he behaves will be part instinctive, where he acts automatically; and part rational, where he thinks about what is happening and then acts accordingly.

Instinctive Actions
These can, from our point of view, be either negative or positive; though the horse will not be making such a distinction.

Positive:- those triggered by his instincts of self-preservation and comfort, such as eating, drinking and seeking the company of other horses.

Negative: - those triggered by his instincts of self-preservation, such as bolting, shying, kicking, biting, rearing, bucking, napping and avoidance of claustrophobic places.

He rarely makes a rational decision to do these, he just feels the need.

Rational Actions
Similarly when he is in his understanding rational mode the results, from our perspective can be positive or negative.

Positive: - he trusts us and our intentions; he understands our signals and follows them to the best of his ability.

Negative: - he decides he does not trust or understand our signals sufficiently so follows our wishes unwillingly, or remembers an unpleasant association and deliberately takes non-compliant action i.e. once previously frightened by a clumsy rider he may have instinctively bucked, now he knows he can dislodge the rider by bucking.

Horses will swing from the instinctive to rational side according to the circumstances. If we want to teach our horse something he must first be in his understanding mode. Then if we repeat our aid or signal exactly the same way each time and he responds in the desired way each time, after a while he no longer has to involve his brain in this process. Communication is through the nervous system so his brain can deal with other things at the same time. A human example would be, whilst learning to drive a car we have to actively think about changing gear and looking in the mirror. Once these skills have been learnt sufficiently we no longer think about driving the car, but can carry on a conversation requiring active thought whilst still driving safely. An equine example might be, that once your horse has learnt to go forward from a light squeeze on his side there is no longer that time gap from giving the signal to him responding, because it is by-passing the brain and communicating through the nervous system. At its lightest he just feels your desire for him to go forward. But when training a new movement you will see in his ears and eyes that he is thinking hard about what is happening between you, and if you reward his try towards the right response, progress will be made. This is why calmness is the first requirement in training.

Therefore establishing a mental connection is of paramount importance if we want our horse to do things willingly. Without the qualities of TRUST, UNDERSTANDING and LEADERSHIP we will not have a willing horse. As these three qualities develop you will see your horse go from:-

Perhaps being downright stubborn.
To just reluctant.
To unreluctant (neutral).
Finally to willing.

How soon this happens will depend on how well you are both connected. This connection is a two way link. Your horse is always telling or asking you something, even if it might appear to be indifference. What he will be showing you will be a reflection of his past experiences with people and situations, and how you appear to him. If you ignore what he is telling you, either deliberately or out of ignorance, you are likely to end up in a confrontation or at best have missed an opportunity to come together. This will dishearten him so that he may not offer it again until the trust and understanding is re-established.

The general scenario for many combinations is not always so extreme because fortunately the horse is, by nature, a very forgiving creature. Many horses will try their hardest for their person, even if the communication is foggy and poorly timed, principally because the trust is there and the horse works out the person's language. What I am trying to present is that if we communicate in a way that approximates how horses communicate with each other, namely through energy and body language, we will have made the important mental connection. Thus we will be tuned in to each other, then I can teach my horse the language to do the tasks I might have in mind. For example the training to be a mounted police horse is very specific and a long way beyond the initial coming together of horse and person, but if we begin by using a language that he understands it will all be accomplished smoother and quicker.

The Physical Connection

This is through your body language which is traditionally known as 'the aids' and generally perceived as pertaining to riding, through the reins, legs, spurs and whips, seat and weight. Rather let us think of body language starting on the ground with your stance, posture and spatial position in relation to that of the horse. These all tell him something because it is how horses communicate with each other. This is how we connect with the horse without touching him or when the rein is deliberately slack. Body language also applies much more specifically through touch. This is the touch of any part of your body which asks him to follow that feel:-

1. Yield to your hand on his skin or through the rein.
2. Yield to your leg.
3. Follow your upper body position.
4. Follow your seat/weight indications.
5. Follow your suggestions.

This physical and mental connection goes hand in hand; the better the one, the better the other. Without a good mental connection the physical expression will be poor, probably tense or dull. On the other hand certain physical movements help the horse to relax and put his mind in a learning state and so improve the mental connection, thus beginning the improving spiral of togetherness.

Feel

The word feel is a good way of describing the relationship between horse and man. It means a direct touch, through your seat, legs and hands. You can feel him and he can feel you. This is the language of the aids and with minor exceptions there is a crude universality about it.

Feel also describes something much less tangible, which by its very definition is hard to put into words. It is:- a perception, an understanding, a sensation, an impression, which is within us physically, mentally, emotionally and spiritually.

We usually describe it in qualitative terms such as:-

'This feels good.'
'This does not feel right.'
'He has little feeling'.
'This feels strange.'
'You have hurt my feelings'.

A horseman, either instinctively, or through awareness developed over time, will pick up a feel from a horse, which tells all. The horse's physical state is an expression that comes from his mind and emotions. At the same time the horse is feeling you. He will know if you are anxious, timid or frightened; even if you have not admitted it to yourself. He will know if you are calm, controlled, and resolute. He will know if you are a leader to look up to and to be with.

So while there is the obvious tangible two way flow of signals between you, there is also this undercurrent of feelings, which is so hard to pinpoint. We all know when it's not right, the difficult part is to correct it and attain that condition where both your minds are reaching for each other for a common purpose. Handling horses with feel raises the experience to a higher plane where the qualities of **willingness, softness, lightness and enjoyment** predominate. This side of horsemanship is rarely articulated and can be best explained by example, which the following case studies attempt to illustrate.

RUTH

Ruth was a bubbly friendly girl; unfortunately due to injury she could not ride her own horse. She kept up her riding by visiting regularly and having lessons on our retired show cob Ben. On this occasion she wanted help with transitions, more especially walk to canter without any trot strides.

After Ruth and Ben had been re-acquainted and warmed up, we started with walk to trot. She found she only obtained trot after a perceptible delay and by lifting her heels and pressing firmly into Ben's side. This was especially frustrating for her since she had seen him perform with invisible aids. Ben was not a machine and her requests needed to be expressed with feel. This is a difficult concept to put across: it is a combination of the physical aids to which the trained horse responds almost as an automatic reflex and the rider's senses – the rider's feeling and the horse's feeling combine to produce the desired movement. This feel comes to some riders instinctively but for most of us it is acquired with practice and experience.

Each horse and rider combination is different. Ben knew the physical aids for trot were a light squeeze of the rider's lower legs. He also had a high opinion of his own worth, and he did not yet feel that Ruth had asked politely or that trot was the desired response. There is a fine line between being ineffective and aggressive. If Ben did not feel connected with his rider and receive clear but light aids he took no notice: if the rider came on too strong he became anxious and over reactive. Ruth needed to quickly convince Ben that she was confident and in control; rather like a teacher silencing an unruly class so that lessons can begin with quiet attentive pupils. I told Ruth she needed to demonstrate to Ben that she could control his speed and direction. I asked her to go round the arena, in rising trot to encourage forward movement. She needed to first 'think forwards' looking at where she wanted to go, then give the light signal with her legs and finally if he did not go from a light signal use her whip behind her leg in a graduated series of taps. The moment he sprang forward all leg action should cease, Ben should maintain the trot of his own accord because of Ruth's feel. Her feel was to project the thought of forwards, not to be tensely pushing with her seat.

Ruth soon found she was riding a different horse; Ben sprang forward drawing on previous hidden reserves of energy. I then asked Ruth to cancel her energy and direct her thoughts to stopping. At first nothing happened because although she had stopped thinking forwards her body was still connected to Ben's energy. I asked her to wiggle her lower jaw and breathe out long and slow. Ben stopped so abruptly she propped onto his neck. How Ben interpreted her 'go and stop' was governed by the feeling and energy she held. With an established partnership this is like a current flowing between the two that can easily be turned up or down.

By the time Ruth had gone around the arena a couple of times, changing gaits between trot, walk and halt, Ben was connected and attentive. Ruth had asked Ben politely but demonstrated she would be as firm as necessary, he instantly sensed her implacable resolve so firmness was no longer needed. She could now concentrate on smoother lighter transitions. Ben was now walking actively, light in hand and flexed at the poll; in other words in the 'ready' position. Ruth thought trot and squeezed with her calves; momentarily Ben gathered, seemed to think better of it, walked another step and ambled into trot. Ruth screamed in frustration, 'I felt he was about to go then it went flat, what happened?' I explained, 'you tightened up at the moment he was going to trot, he felt it in your seat, body, legs and hands. That was enough to stop him following your thought and lightest of aids so he waited for the more solid command of a stronger leg aid, by then the flow and lightness had evaporated.'

Ruth was becoming increasingly frustrated, blaming herself and worrying that she was ruining Ben. I suggested she should see this as a learning process and not to expect perfection straightaway. She was trying too hard, and this in itself was preventing it happening. Instead let Ben help her. So she rode round the arena going from walk to trot and back to walk every five yards. Horses, especially a sensitive intelligent one like Ben, soon pick up a pattern and will offer to help the rider to become softer as they know what is expected from following the pattern. By the time Ruth had executed a dozen of these transitions she was doing very little. She stopped and I encouraged her to describe what she felt had happened between her and Ben.

'Well', she said, 'the first few upward transitions were wooden and rough, but I did not mind because you said that was likely to happen. As Ben got into it I could feel him waiting for my signal so I did not worry that he was not going to do it, then it only took a light squeeze. In the end all I was doing was just thinking I wanted to trot. It's great.' She beamed, smiling for the first time.

I then told her how it had looked from the ground. Initially there had been the tense upward transition when she had tightened her body and lifted up her heels. This gave way to a more relaxed confident expectation as Ben began to help her. I could see she believed Ben would trot, so her lower back softened and her hip joints opened because of the release of the previously tensed muscles. This softening travelled down to her knee, which no longer gripped, and onto her heel which as a result did not lift up as she gave the signal with her calf muscle. Also as she felt the certainty that Ben would trot she waited for it to happen. Her thought and belief in herself and in Ben had caused micro muscular alterations readily received by her horse. Previously she had been giving herself instructions such as 'don't look down', 'don't grip', and 'heels down'. These were by and large negative, specific and rational directions which by there very nature were counter productive. Instead, letting go of these thoughts, and seeing in her mind the bigger picture of a trot transition, had connected with Ben much more clearly than the mechanical physical aids. I told her that now she was riding with 'feel'. How she was inside, her thoughts, beliefs, intentions were a greater and more powerful influence than she had realised.

The next step was the walk to canter transition. Again the burden of a new, and in Ruth's mind a harder task, brought back her habit of trying too hard and tightening. Consequently Ben put in a few intervening trot strides. When a horse goes straight from walk to canter he momentarily gathers his energy, balancing himself so as to push both forward and up into the first canter stride. Ben had thoroughly learnt the generally accepted canter aids of outside leg slightly back, inside leg pushing forward on the girth. What was needed was an over riding feel and timing to produce a smooth flowing movement into canter.

Ruth tried a series of walk to canter transitions; some were instantaneous which brought squeals of glee. She knew straight away when it was not going to work and no longer worried or kicked at Ben. I suggested she view the transition as missing out a gear when changing up in a car. One would only go straight from second to fourth gear if the engine had built up enough 'revs' in the first place. For the horse this is an increase in energy which he easily brings about if he is stimulated by fear, excitement or inclination. Without such stimulation the rider has to first bring up their energy. A rider with a good seat is already connected with their horse, riding the wave of his movement, not hindering the flow. A change in the rider's flow and energy, almost imperceptible to an onlooker, will be immediately felt by the horse. Then the rider has to only release this energy by allowing a little with the hands for the horse to go straight into canter.

I asked Ruth to look out into the world, to be aware of what was around her. To help with bringing up her energy I asked her to think of a beach ball in her stomach which she could lift up and toss over Ben's ears. Any looking down, leaning forward, and closing of her chest would stifle the energy and send it into the ground: then Ben could only respond to her leg aids a fraction of a second later having lost the rolling wave of energy. This in turn would require a greater physical effort, making the transition appear ponderous or with intermediary trot strides. When it worked well for Ruth she said she just thought canter; she felt Ben gather himself up, then she opened her chest, gave the tinniest of leg aids and he popped into canter - like squeezing a wet bar of soap.

Sometimes it did not happen for a split second after her request, at others immediately. This was because Ben's legs were not in the right place to respond. Ruth asked if she should give the aid when a certain shoulder was back to facilitate the transition. My answer was both yes and no. So long as she did not have to look down or consciously think 'where is each shoulder', yes give the thought and aid at that point. But if she started concentrating on each shoulder, her timing and softness would be affected and so would the transition. Ruth's general awareness of Ben's movement and balance needed to be developed to the point where she was receiving a constant flow of information, which she could absorb with her senses, without consciously thinking about it. Then she would discover that her thought and aids for the canter transition (her feel) would coincide with the right moment for Ben.

At the end of the lesson Ruth felt that joy and frustration common to all riders. The ecstasy of the few perfect transitions, where she and Ben acted as one: this was tempered with the frustration of losing the feel and timing. Unlike sports which do not include another living creature, Ruth could not practice indefinitely until she got it right. Ben had only a certain number of transitions he would be prepared to perform before fatigue and boredom set in. Feel is the essence of horsemanship, where ultimately the horse is responsible for the quality of execution, which gives the 'highs' a unique poignancy. Having tasted the fruit of riding with feel Ruth wanted more but, she had learnt that trying too hard destroyed the connection with Ben. The old saying that 'less is more' was very apt in this lesson.

SUE

While Ruth developed her depth of feel in a specific exercise, Sue needed help in a wider sphere. Her difficulties lay in hacking out. Riding a horse alone on today's roads is a very great challenge. Training a horse to be steady in traffic requires experience, tact, self-awareness and self-discipline; in short all the qualities of leadership needed by a horseman.

Sue's horse Tammy was a highly intelligent Iberian mare, always interested in what was happening. Her actions and reactions were varied, volatile and unpredictable. Just what you would expect from a horse bred to survive in the bull ring. In Tammy's case they had not yet been trained, honed and smoothed into a specific purpose. One second she would be calmly trotting along, the next leaping about like a cat. None of this was deliberately aimed against Sue; it was just what she felt she had to do at that particular moment. However traumatic the ride Tammy held no grudges and afterwards was always friendly and eager to be with Sue. It was impossible not to love Tammy but she did at times drive Sue to distraction, especially out hacking. She soon settled to hacking out with another older horse, often taking the lead; she would spook at the odd thing in the hedge but was reasonably behaved for a young inexperienced horse. However on her own Sue often could not get her more than fifty yards from the stable. When Tammy did get going she might stop dead at the sight of a cow in the distance. Some cars and lorries she would ignore, others she would not go past.

I explained to Sue that Tammy had a highly developed sense of self-preservation, combined with the athleticism to instantly take care of herself. Leaving the yard was leaving her herd and security: it was different in the company of other horses, then she was part of the herd and felt secure. Every step further from home heightened her fears, which were compounded if Sue became cross and urged her on. This often resulted in Tammy shooting backwards at high speed. Every strange object became a source of potential danger. In this state she was likely to leap in front of a car, to get away from the flapping bag in the hedge. The answer lay in presenting leadership, and going out often enough so Tammy became familiarized to the dangers of the outside world.

Sue needed to build a connection where she became Tammy's leader, taking on the role of the older calmer horse. Tammy needed to feel, accept and desire her leadership, so she need no longer feel totally responsible for her own safety. Thus when Tammy felt insecure Sue need only quietly and re-assuringly close her legs and gently feel on the reins; just as a mother would hold a child's hand for comfort. Sue had such a connection on the ground. She had taught Tammy to lead really well from both sides; she could halt and back up with the slightest of touches and suggestions. Tammy would bend easily, yield her hind and fore quarters and move sideways with equal facility. She would circle on the lunge at walk, trot and canter, with good transitions and changes of rein. In short Tammy's level of obedience and manners on the ground were much to be envied. Sue really did feel that she was in charge, as a good leader she kept Tammy's work interesting and varied so it became more of a game than a chore.

In the saddle Sue did not present Tammy with the same secure feeling; partly because she was not experienced riding young horses and partly due to stiffness from an old back injury. Understandably Sue felt less confident in the saddle than on the ground. Tammy knew this, so she resumed responsibility for her own safety. Sue's job was to put herself in a position where she would feel confident and in control. To increase Tammy's familiarization Sue led her out in hand. This was a great way to accustom her to traffic which was so essential on today's busy roads.

Sue also led Tammy around some of the hacking routes. On returning she said, 'she's much happier if I walk slightly in front, if I'm by her shoulder she's hesitant.' This was because Tammy was prepared to follow Sue into possible danger but not be driven into it where her nose became the pathfinder. This also approximates the rider's position when mounted, sitting up there driving the horse on. This is why when you dismount and lead your horse he usually follows like a lamb.

Sue's next step, after leading out, was to mount and ride the last half mile home. By then Tammy was relaxed, eager to go home and a little tired (so was Sue after all that walking). This was a win win situation for both of them. Gradually Sue rode for longer, but it was by no means straight forward. Tammy would sometimes still not

CONNECTING – FEEL

This horse is being exposed to traffic and reacts violently. I am placed between him and the road which is the safest position for me and the most re-assuring for him.

Ten minutes later he is becoming much calmer.

leave the yard and out on the ride Sue would have to dismount if she stopped completely. It is not a weakness on the rider's part if they dismount to negotiate a tricky section and then get on again. It is better to avoid a confrontation if you are not certain you can win. Some people would use the whip strongly to send the horse forward. Those sort of people convey an implacable self-belief which the horse will feel and will often respond by going forward. But if your conviction is not made of steel, your horse will sense this and take little notice despite the physical pain. I advised Sue that when Tammy stopped, just to sit there and wait, allowing Tammy to check out the situation: often this in itself is enough. Any urging forward has to be so low key that it is just thinking forward with only light leg aids. Or put another way: repeatedly asking politely rather than shouting, which can be counter-productive. It is as if the connection between horse and rider is elastic; it will stretch but too much force will make it snap. It also helped Sue if she moved over Tammy's quarters with a leg and rein aid on the same side. This bending movement often unlocks the front end. This also showed Tammy that Sue could move her, even if it was not initially where she wanted to go.

As the weeks went by Sue felt she was gaining the upper hand. She also felt she had some strategies to fall back on when Tammy stopped or whirled round or backed up. Depending on the circumstances i.e. the level of traffic, the danger of ditches or holes etc., she could;-

Wait and passively go with Tammy, ignoring the behaviour.
Turn her round sharply in small circles, thus directing the excess energy into movement of her choosing.
Get off and do some groundwork to re-establish the mental connection so Tammy was focused on her.

However these strategies were only a response to Tammy's behaviour. Sue was like a tennis player returning the ball but not winning the game. I suggested Sue view the world outside the yard as just a bigger schooling arena. I did not want her to hack out as if riding a dressage test, but often people totally change their way of riding outside the arena. To some riding in the arena is formal and regimented, a place of education and total control; whilst outside it the riding is informal and relaxing. How much nicer it is, if in the arena, there are plenty of times when the horse is ridden on a long rein and allowed to be at ease; perhaps even ridden with no reins and bareback. Similarly out hacking why not occasionally, space permitting, stop and practice some obedience and suppling movements. Five minutes spent on turns on the forehand, pirouettes, lateral work, halting and backing can re-tune horse and rider. It need only be at the walk, nothing too energetic or excitable. So during a one and a half hour ride, two or three five minute sessions can be very beneficial. Conversely, during an hour in the arena similar short breaks will help to keep your horse sweet.

Sue began to give Tammy some jobs to do out hacking. She would ride to the cross-country course, dismount and jump Tammy, on line, over some of the fences. This gave them both a sense of purpose, enhancing their communication and togetherness. At other times she practiced leg yielding across the track. All these things increased Sue's belief that she could influence her horse, and Tammy's confidence to accept and rely on Sue's guidance.

Leaving the yard was the last big challenge. To a certain extent the initial insecurity had turned into a game where Tammy would test Sue's resolve. However being such a mercurial horse, if Sue became too reactionary to the playing up, the problem would escalate out of hand to the point where both parties went into self-preservation mode. In this scenario I advised Sue to see herself like an angler trying to land a big fish. She needed to alternate letting the line out and reeling in; otherwise the line or the hook might break. Her reeling in was when she politely but firmly asked Tammy to forward: her letting out was when she went with Tammy's reactions, going with her until that little tantrum had expired then politely asking her to go forward again.

Luckily Sue had great patience and persistence, being prepared to take the time needed. She knew her own abilities, her strengths and weaknesses and worked with and around them. This was despite other people offering advice and telling her how they would 'sort the horse out'. Over a period of two years Sue reached the point where she could hack out on her own with only an occasional blip and re-occurrence of Tammy's insecurity. This might seem a long time but Sue was typical of the majority of working riders. Tammy's time with her had to be juggled with her job, holidays and the general flotsam that is thrown up in life. During a year they would only manage a few hours riding a week. At the end of two years the connection between them was strong, consistent and above all happy.

CHRISTIAN. Thus being launched again into the gulf of misery, unless a miracle of grace prevent it, they everlastingly perish in their own deceivings.
(The Pilgrim's Progress – John Bunyan)

His sole experiences of horse sales had been Tattersalls at Newmarket, where the crème de la crème of equine aristocrats were sold for tens and even hundred of thousands. Then he had been a lowly stud hand, content to watch in awe. Now was different; starting as a fledgling 'horse coper' he needed stock of his own, to make money, enhance his reputation and broaden his experience. Hence on a cold November day he found himself at a sale of 'Racehorses out of training and others'. This was distinctly down market, comprising a few quality animals sprinkled amongst the no hopers and the has-beens, all purebred or at least seven eighths. He hoped there might be something which was not quite good enough to race but would make a riding horse. The catalogue was of little use for him, apart from giving the horse's age; it aptly concentrated on pedigree and racing performance. Wandering through the yards, where the two hundreds lots were stabled, only increased his confusion. It was easy to pick out the stars by the throng of people at the stable doors, but finding a bargain amongst the rest was proving tricky.

He watched the first twenty lots go through the ring, to see if there was a pattern in the prices and to get a feel of the ring; it terrified him. He did not know if he would have the nerve to stick his hand up even if he saw a horse he wanted. The cheaper horses were always at the beginning and the end of the sale, so far there had only been two in his price range of £700. One was a three year old that had never raced with terrible curby hocks; the other a four year old out of training that had run only four times, looked thin and was sold without warranty. It went for the meat price. The reality at the bottom end of the racing industry was depressing. He cautiously raised his hand for Lot 35, a big unbacked three year old, obviously not fast enough for flat racing. He waved again; the auctioneer took no notice concentrating on two rival bidders until one of them dropped out. Then he turning in his direction he asked,

'Is that a bid sir?' peering intimidatingly over his spectacles.

He hastily lowered his hand and shook his head; the price had gone over his limit. The horse was eventually knocked down to a chasing trainer, standing near the auctioneer, for £2500.

By the afternoon and Lot 170 he was becoming desperate; no longer shy at bidding he had failed to get within reach of buying anything. Meanwhile the auctioneer's voice casually droned on. It seemed selling horses required a slow measured voice, the dearer the horse the more casual the tone: whereas at the cattle markets the dearer the beast the more frantic the auctioneer. The next in was Lot 192.

'Two year old chestnut filly……. related to Sir Ivor on the dam's side and going back to Aureole on the sire's …….. been given time to mature, ready to race next season. What am I bid gentlemen, 800 for this fine filly, well 600, 300 to start then?' The auctioneer drawled with little enthusiasm.

The bidding stuck at 600, he cautiously raised his hand. This time, with little other interest, he was spotted immediately.

'620 in the stands', was the quick reply. The next words he heard were, '680 on the market, selling in the stands'. Then the hammer came down, he had bought the horse, he gave his name and address to the assistant; it was done. Only then did it sink in that until the auctioneer had said 'on the market' the horse had not reached its reserve, furthermore with the speed which the hammer came down he must have been the only bidder. 680 was within his limit, except of course these horses were being sold in guineas so he ended up paying £714, which was not so good.

He made his way through the now deserted yards, most of the horses had already departed. At box 192 he saw a chestnut head weaving from side to side. It was time to go home.

He knew he had been foolish, made all the classic mistakes at an auction, but he liked his little chestnut filly. Back home, in daylight he could see she was small, only 15hands. She had looked bigger in the ring, but then he had been up in the stands where it is difficult to gauge the height: the professional bidders always stood at the entrance, where they were on the same level as the horses.

Ginny, as he called her, soon settled into the routine of out in the field by day and in the stable at night. She weaved less in the stable with the low walls where she could see and touch the horses either side. Any change in routine or excitement would start her off again. His plan was to let her have the winter to settle, back her in late spring then sell her at the end of the summer as 'lightly ridden away'. He would rather have bought a three year old which he could have sold on after a year, ready for more serious work. However he had Ginny, so the best he could do was make sure he did a good job of backing her and hopefully she would have grown by next year.

This optimism was dented when his teacher and mentor came to visit. It was not so much what she said but rather what she did not say that disturbed him. Instead of praising him for his eye for a horse and what a useful type he had bought, all she said was,

'She's got a pretty little head; you'll have fun breaking this one'.

Ginny wintered well, so come May he started her training in earnest. He did not have an arena, just the cobbled yard or the corner of the 3 acre paddock. This had proved ample for those he had backed up until now. Ginny was different, she became agitated when he took her away from the other horses in the field or away from her stable. Even leading her up and down the farmyard would set her off, and it was within 20yards of the other horses but out of their sight. She would jog and prance around whinnying loudly. Lungeing in the field was a nightmare. He fenced the corner off with some jump stands and poles; it was the only way to stop her dragging him all over the field. As it was she would only walk if he held her close, otherwise she would race round and round at the end of the lunge line. He could tire her out until she trembled, lathered in sweat and her eyes bulged with fear; but this was counter productive as she would go off her food and it took several days of gentle handling to get her back to normal.

The horseman had taught him how to back a youngster and it had served him well until now. The procedure was straight forward. The first two weeks began with grooming and handling in the stable, then teaching to lead in hand followed by lungeing. After quietly mounting for the first time an assistant led the horse round, this progressed to being lunged. Gradually the assistant did less until you were completely in charge and let off the lunge. By the end of a month you and the horse could walk, trot and canter in the arena. The horseman would adapt and adjust the system to meet each individual horse's needs: what would he have done with Ginny?

He stopped the lungeing and any thoughts of backing her, or even taking her away from the other horses, while he thought what to do next. Ginny's main problem was her insecurity; when away from the other horses she would become hysterical and uncontrollable. Her breeding for the racetrack encouraged her instincts to run at the slightest stimulation. On the other hand a regular routine instilled security and comfort; Ginny's routine was to be with the other horses not with him. Anything he did with her, apart from taking her to and from the field, was too big a step from what she knew. He decided he had to develop her trust in him and proceed at her pace, not follow a set procedure: he must be flexible.

He reasoned the most comfortable place for her was in the stable where she could see the other horses. So anything new was first introduced in the stable, starting with the saddle and bridle. He took plenty of time, rubbing her with the saddle, letting her sniff it and taking it on and off many times without even thinking of doing up the girth. After a week she was introduced to being girthed, again this was tightened up hole by hole over several sessions. The next step was to lead her round the farmyard, three or four times a day until it became part of her routine. Gradually she would allow herself to be led further away from the yard before she started to whinny. He just ignored this as if nothing had happened; frequently stopping to let her graze the sweet untouched grass on the side of the track. Her zone of trust grew to several hundred yards and lasted twenty minutes. The most secure place for her was still the stable, so this is where he decided to back her and do it on his own.

He reasoned it had taken so long for her to trust him how much longer to trust a second person? Also with two people her attention would be divided, whereas he wanted it all on himself. After a successful walk round the farm he quietly mounted her in the stable, soothing and talking to her gently. It felt strange sitting up there, the stable seemed very small, the top of the walls very close. If she bucked or threw herself around he would be scraped on the wall or worse tipped over it into the adjoining box. It was an act of faith; she trusted him, now he had to trust her. After only ten long seconds he slid to the ground; she had been wary but trusting, he had been anxious but quietly confident.

After that progress was relatively rapid. Still each new step was first introduced and then consolidated before moving onto something new. Ginny's reactions dictated the speed of progress. First he moved around in the saddle, still stroking and talking to her. Next he bent her head around, moved one step and dismounted. Progressing slowly but surely it took a month to get to riding round the farm, both with other horses and by herself. If he missed a day it took the whole of the next session to get back to where they had been. If he missed two days it took even longer. Ginny needed the routine, to be re-assured that things were the same day in day out. By the end of the summer it was time for her to be sold.

He was not happy to part with her but her could not justify keeping her; she had been an investment to make money. He toyed with the idea of giving her another year with a view to selling her as a potential competition horse. The reality was she was too small, now only 15.1hh. She would be too sensitive and excitable for most teenagers and not big or good enough for an experienced horseman. Plus there would be the expense of keeping her for another year, with no guarantee he would get any more for her as a four year old. More tellingly, if he was going to pursue this career he must learn to harden his heart and be able to sell a horse.

Ginny was advertised in the local paper.

'15.1 TB chestnut filly 3yrs lightly backed ready to go on, £1000.'

There were only two phone calls, one from a lady inquiring if she was traffic proof and suit a novice rider. He could not lie, he had to say she had only been on very quiet roads and was not for an inexperienced rider. The other caller sounded more hopeful, wanting to come and try her out. He looked like an ex jockey, small with a thin pinched face. He did not like the look of him nor the way he rode. He never spoke to or patted Ginny, holding her in much shorter than usual. The longer he rode the more the horse became agitated, flicking her ears and rolling her eyes. Luckily he stopped before she reached boiling point.

'She's a bit nervous, isn't she lad, she'll need a lot more work? I could take her off your hands for £650,' the man offered.

Quickly turning down this offer he could not wait for this horrible man to leave.

The man's parting words were,

'Well you have got my number if you change your mind, and I see she weaves as well.'

It took both he and Ginny several days to get rid of the taste of this experience. It seemed there was only a demand for proven riding horses, preferably five or six years old; or for quality youngsters with greater potential than Ginny. He carried on riding her, but he could not bring himself to hold her in tight and give her the appearance of being more advanced. He had his principles; Ginny was a green three year old that should only be lightly ridden on a long rein and preferably turned away until next year to mature. Unfortunately for him much of the rest of the horse world did not see it like that; his principles were going to cost him dear.

As the end of summer approached, with still no interest in Ginny, he took the hard decision to put her back in the sale where he had bought her. He reasoned with himself that there would be more potential buyers gathered together, so the chances of someone wanting her would be increased. He ignored the quiet whisper in his head that said 'you have no control over who might buy her; it might be a dealer like the one you turned away. Once the hammer's down, that's it.'

Being a seller at the sale was very different from being a buyer. A year ago he had felt keyed up with an apprehensive but excited tingle inside. He had felt important about to make a purchase. Now he was just apprehensive, staying in or near Ginny's stable. This was not just to woo potential buyers, but to calm Ginny so she did not weave. The atmosphere of the sales had brought out all her old anxieties. All vices like weaving had to be declared and the auctioneer would announce it from the rostrum; however there was no need for people to know any sooner than that. Also he hoped people might miss it in the excitement, not the professionals but maybe Ginny would be bought by somebody who was as nice and as naïve as he had been.

People walked along past the boxes looking at the lots for sale, occasionally pulling out a horse to see it walk and trot up the aisle. It was very depressing; few buyers looked closely at Ginny; most just glanced over the top door, looked at the catalogue and walked on. When he had been a buyer he had felt excited, now he just felt anxious that she might not sell at all. To make matters worse the auctioneer, on inspecting Ginny, had suggested he lower his reserve if he did not want to take her home again. Reluctantly he followed this advice, not wishing to waste the transport and entry costs. By the time he brought her out to parade in the collecting ring, prior to selling, only two people had seemed genuinely interested. He really hoped the pleasant couple from Hereford bought Ginny. She behaved well in the collecting ring; he kept her walking to calm her nerves and his. He could have ridden her round but had decided not to in case she played up; now he was regretting this decision, it might have brought more interest.

His turn was late in the afternoon near the end of the sale. Thankfully the ring was still full of people, although nothing like what it had been two hours earlier when the top lots had gone through. The auctioneer read out Ginny's details; age, pedigree and experience whilst he walked her around the ring which seemed very small and the people very close. His stomach churned. As usual the auctioneer opened at near the reserve price, only rarely was there a bid at this, so the bidding would start at a much lower price and would with luck climb back up to and beyond the reserve. It was a shock that she started at 300 and climbed so slowly as he walked round and round. He had dropped the reserve down to 800, much less than the 1000 he had wanted. The bidding hung at 780 for a whole lap of the ring; finally the hammer fell at 800. It was over; he led Ginny out of the ring to the sound of the auctioneer dispassionately introducing the next lot. He was sweating, feeling weak with relief and disappointment. Seeing the couple from Hereford he asked, 'did you buy her?' 'No we bought one half an hour ago', was the reply. He felt a quiet unease, he had been pinning his hopes on them. The buyer was just a name 'Watson' on the transport slip.

The last he saw of Ginny, she was being led away for loading, he did not want to look anymore. The sale ring was not a place for the squeamish.

A picture can only be really appreciated when it is finished; until then the direction, style and meaning can be altered. The first few strokes show the subject; the last only really bring it to life. Horses were his obsession but he did not much

A HORSEMAN'S PROGRESS

like the look of his painting so far. In his interview for the job with the horseman he had been given a glimpse of the trials and tribulations that lay ahead. To succeed, he had been told, one needed either wealth or talent, preferably both. A horseman's reputation was his greatest asset, which took a long time to build but could be ruined with a few thoughtless acts.

Driving back from the sale he thought of these sage words and imagined what his venerated teacher would say to him now.

'You went to a public sale to buy a horse to sell on and make money? Was it a good quality horse, was it what you intended to buy?'

'No, I shouldn't have gone and no she wasn't what I was looking for.'

'Was the breaking and schooling easy? Was it a quick turn around? Was it easy to sell her, was there a market?'

'No', again he had to confess.

'Well what have you learnt from this fruitless exercise?' his mentor's voice echoed in his head.

He reflected in the mirror of the horseman's censure.

Ginny had apparently sold for nearly a hundred more than he had paid, but with commission the difference was only £28. Include the transport costs and her keep for a year he must have lost several hundred pounds. He would never make money this way. His reputation which was still embryonic in the locality had gained nothing by this venture. The only plus he could see was that he had furthered his experience handling a difficult horse. Then he could have offered to break in a horse for free, to gain experience and still not been out of pocket. Perhaps most unpleasant was the aftertaste that he had not done his best for Ginny. If he was truthful part of him had been glad to see her go, turning a blind eye to where she might end up. However much he might say, 'it was just business', he knew it was not right. He was not cut out to buy and sell horses, that needed a thick skin.

During the next year he broke and schooled a few local horses, keeping well away from any horse sales. This was the direction in which he felt most comfortable; there was not much money in it; there never has been with horses. Occasionally he would open that small box deep within his heart and wonder what had happened to Ginny.

More than a year after she had gone he got a phone call.

'I have got a chestnut filly, rising five I hope you might be able to tell me something about her?'

He felt weak as his conscience flooded in, but grew stronger as he learnt more.

'We bought her from a riding school that got her off a dealer. Apparently she did not settle at that but she suits us down to the ground. We just have the three horses and she is just what my wife wanted, she is lively but controllable so long as you're sensitive like her. She fits in here really well; I could see she had been started right by someone.'

A miracle of grace had occurred.

Selected bibliography

I have read and enjoyed many books about horsemanship, too many to list them all. So I am limiting myself to a dozen that have struck a cord for me, in the chronological order in which they were read.

My Horses My Teachers - Alois Podhajsky

Dressage - Henry Wynmalen

Horse Training, Outdoor and High School - Etienne Beaudant

The Reforming of Dangerous and Useless Horses - Mike Rimington

Complete Training of Horse and Rider - Alois Podhajsky

Understanding Equitation - Jean Saint-Fort Paillard

Centered Riding - Sally Swift

The Way to Perfect Horsemanship - Udo Berger

Natural Horse-man-ship - Pat Parelli

The Art of Training - Hans Blixen-Finecke

True Horsemanship Through Feel - Bill Dorrence and Leslie Desmond

What Horses Reveal - Klaus Ferdinand Hempfling

Printed in the United Kingdom
by Lightning Source UK Ltd.
129560UK00001B/205-252/A